fun & funky | knitting

fun & funky knitting

30 EASY ACCESSORIES TO INSPIRE

Emma King

COLLINS & BROWN

First published in the United Kingdom 2006 by
Collins & Brown
10 Southcombe Street
London
W14 0RA

An imprint of Anova Books Company Ltd

ISBN 978-1-84340-296-1

A CIP catalogue record for this book is available from
the British Library.

10 9 8 7 6 5 4 3

Reproduction by Anorax
Printed by Craft Print International Ltd, Singapore

Keep updated. Email crafts@anovabooks.com for
FREE email alerts on forthcoming titles.

This book can be ordered direct from the publisher.
Contact the marketing department, but try your
bookshop first.

www.anovabooks.com

contents

introduction

Knitted accessories are fun to make and give you a chance to experiment with colours and yarns to create eye-catching designs. This collection of accessories, my second book, includes hats, scarves, bags and even some jewellery meaning you will never be without a little knitted something to brighten up your wardrobe!

Projects range from big chunky bags and belts to delicate knits using fine yarns, beads and even wire. Whilst working through these projects you will have the chance to try out techniques and learn new skills such as knitting with beads, stitch work and colourwork.

Colour is the inspiration behind all my designs. There are so many wonderful yarns and shades available that I am never without a new combination or idea to try out! I hope that by following the patterns in this book and working with my palette and yarn choices, you will also try out some yarn and colour combinations of your own. In some of my designs I have used finishing touches such as knitted flowers, frills and twisted cords for extra fun! All these are quick, simple additions that can embellish many projects or outfits so why not make a "Petal Corsage" for every day of the week. One in pinks, one in greens, one in purples…the possibilities are endless!

I hope you have fun knitting these designs and find inspiration to keep on knitting and accessorising!

emma king

yarns and materials

Choosing the right yarn

If you want your accessories to look like the pictures in the book, I would recommend that you use the yarns that I have specified for each design. A substitute yarn that differs in weight, shade, or fiber content will change the whole look, feel, and size of the finished bag.

Quantities and dye lots

At the beginning of each project the quantities of yarn are given for the bag. If different yarns are used, these quantities will alter. This is because the length of a ball of yarn depends on its weight and fiber content: an aran weight cotton will have a shorter length than an aran weight wool, and a 4-ply cotton will have a longer length than a double-knit cotton. The quantities of yarn can be re-calculated if desired. Buy all the yarn you need to complete the project at the same time, checking the ball bands to ensure that all the balls are from the same dye lot. The colour of a specific shade of yarn can vary quite a lot between dye lots and the change will show in the finished project.

Yarn used in this book

A selection of yarns from the Rowan Yarn collection have been used to knit all of the designs in this book. Following is a guide to the yarns used.

II Seasons Cotton

Aran-weight cotton and microfiber yarn
60% cotton/40% microfiber
Approximately 90 m (98 yd) per 50 g (1¾ oz) ball

Big Wool

Super chunky pure wool
100% merino wool
Approximately 80 m (87 yd) per 100 g (3½ oz) ball

Calmer

Soft cotton mix
75% cotton/25% acrylic/microfiber
Approximately 160 m (175 yd) per 50 g (1¾ oz) ball

Chunky Print

Chunky pure wool
100% wool
Approximately 100 m (109 yd) per 100 g (3½ oz) ball

Cotton Glacé

Lightweight cotton yarn
100% cotton
Approximately 115 m (125 yd) per 50 g (1¾ oz) ball

Felted Tweed
Lightweight double knitting
50% merino wool/25% alpaca/25% viscose
Approximately 175 m (191 yd) per 50 g
(1³/₄ oz) ball

Handknit DK Cotton
Medium-weight cotton yarn
100% cotton
Approximately 85 m (92 yd) per 50 g (1³/₄ oz) ball

Kid Classic
Aran weight mohair mix
70% lambswool/26% kid mohair/ 4% nylon
Approximately 140 m (153 yd) per 50 g
(1³/₄ oz) ball

Kid Silk Haze
Very lightweight mohair yarn
70% super kid mohair/30% silk
Approximately 210 m (230 yd) per 25 g (1 oz) ball

Lurex Shimmer
Very lightweight lurex yarn
80% viscose/20% polyester
Approximately 95 m (104 yd) per 25 g (1 oz) ball

Plaid
Chunky wool mix
42% merino wool/30% Acrylic fibre/28%
Superfine alpaca
Approximately 100 m (109 yd) per 100 g
(3¹/₂ oz) ball

Ribbon Twist
Super Chunky
70% wool/25% Acrylic/5% Polyamide
Approximately 60 m (66 yd) per 100 g (3¹/₂ oz) ball

Rowan Denim
Medium-weight cotton yarn
100% cotton
Approximately 93 m (101 yd) per 1³/₄ oz (50 g) ball

Summer Tweed
Aran-weight silk and cotton yarn
70% silk/30% cotton
Approximately 108 m (118 yd) per 50 g
(1³/₄ oz) hank

Wool Cotton
Double-knitting-weight wool and cotton
50% merino wool/50% cotton
Approximately 113 m (123 yd) per 50 g
(1³/₄ oz) ball

Yorkshire Tweed 4ply
4ply pure wool
100% pure new wool
Approximately 110 m (120 yd) per 25 g (1 oz) ball

Yorkshire Tweed DK
Double knitting pure wool
100% pure new wool
Approximately 113 m (123 yd) per 50 g
(1³/₄ oz) ball

4-ply Soft
Fine pure wool
100% merino wool
Approximately 175 m (191 yd) per 50 g
(1³/₄ oz) ball

4ply Cotton
4ply pure cotton
100% Cotton
Approximately 170 m (186 yd) per 50 g
(1³/₄ oz) ball

working from a pattern

Before starting any pattern, always read it through. This will give you an idea of how the design is structured and the techniques that are involved. Each pattern includes the following elements.

Materials

This section gives a list of materials required, including the amount of yarn, sizes of needles and any buttons or zippers. The yarn amounts quoted are based on average requirements and are therefore approximate.

Abbreviations

Knitting instructions are normally given in an abbreviated form which saves valuable space. In this book the most commonly used abbreviations are listed on page 11 and additional abbreviations specific to a project are listed on the project page.

Garment instructions

Before starting to knit, read the instructions carefully to understand the abbreviations used, how the design is structured, and in which order each piece is worked. However, there may be some parts of the pattern that only become clear when you are knitting them, so do not assume that you are being slow or that the pattern is wrong.

Asterisks or brackets are used to indicate the repetition of a sequence of stitches. For example: *K3, P1; rep from * to end. This means, knit three stitches, then purl one stitch, then repeat this sequence to the end of the row. It could also be written: [K3, P1] to end. Asterisks and brackets may be used together in a row. For example: *K4, P1, [K1, P1] 3 times; rep from * to end. The part of the

instruction in brackets indicates that these stitches only are to be repeated three times before returning to the instructions immediately after the asterisk.

When repeating anything, make sure that you are doing so the correct number of times. For example: [K1, P1] twice means that 4 stitches are worked, but *K1, P1; rep from * twice more means 6 stitches are worked.

The phrase 'work straight' means continue without increasing or decreasing the number of stitches and keeping the established pattern correct.

When you put your knitting aside, always mark where you are on the pattern; it is better to be safe than sorry, especially if a complex stitch is involved.

If the figure 0 appears within an instruction, for example, 'K1(0:1:2) sts.' this means that for that particular size no stitches are worked at that point. Take special care if the sizes have been separated for a particular instruction. For example, suppose that the pattern states '1st and 4th sizes only Cast off 15(20) sts, work to end.'. For the 1st size, follow the instructions outside the round brackets, and for the 4th size follow those within them. For any other size, these instructions do not apply.

Making up

The Making up section in each project will tell you how to join the knitted pieces together. Always follow the recommended sequence.

Gauge (tension) and selecting correct needle size

The needle sizes that I have recommended for each design have been chosen to create a firm gauge (tension). This is especially important if you are knitting accessories that are going to be handled, such as bags. If the knitting is too loose, the article will easily become misshapen, and will most likely drop and grow in size. Using a slightly smaller needle than the usual recommended size for the yarn ensures that the knitted fabric retains its shape.

Gauge (tension) can differ quite dramatically between knitters. This is because of the way that the needles and the yarn are held. So if your gauge (tension) does not match that stated in the pattern, you should change your needle size following this simple rule:

- If your knitting is too loose, your gauge (tension) will read that you have less stitches and rows than the given gauge (tension), and you will need to change to a thinner needle to make the stitch size smaller.
- If your knitting is too tight, your gauge (tension) will read that you have more stitches

and rows than the given gauge (tension), and you will need to change to a thicker needle to make the stitch size bigger.

Please note that if the projects in this book are not knitted to the correct gauge (tension), yarn quantities will be affected.

Knitting a gauge swatch

No matter how excited you are about a new knitting project and how annoying it seems to have to spend time knitting up a gauge swatch before you start, please do take the time, as it will not be wasted.

Use the same needles, yarn and stitch pattern as those that will be used for the main work and knit a sample at least 12.5 cm (5 in) square. Smooth out the finished piece on a flat surface, but do not stretch it.

To check the stitch gauge, place a ruler horizontally on the sample, measure 10 cm (4 in) across and mark with a pin at each end. Count the number of stitches between the pins. To check the row gauge, place a ruler vertically on the sample, measure 10 cm (4 in) and mark with pins. Count the number of rows between the pins. If the number of stitches and rows is greater then specified in the pattern, make a new swatch using larger needles; if it is less, make a new swatch using smaller needles.

abbreviations

beg	beginning/begin		work between the needle points and wrap around your thumb to create loop and then back through the needle points. Now, knit into the stitch again and then slip off needle. You will now have two stitches on the right hand needle. Cast one off by lifting one over the other.
cont	continue		
cm	centimetre		
c4b	cable 4 back: slip next 2 sts onto a cable needle and hold at back of work, k2, then k2 from the cable needle		
c4f	cable 4 front: slip next 2 sts onto a cable needle and hold at front of work, k2, then k2 from the cable needle	oz	ounces
		p	purl
c6b	cable 6 back: slip next 3 sts onto a cable needle and hold at back of work, k3, then k3 from the cable needle	p2sso	pass two slipped stitches over
		p2togtbl	purl 2 stitches together through the back of the loop
		patt	pattern
dec	decrease	pb	place bead: yarn forward, slip bead to front of work, slip 1 st purlwise, take yarn to back of work. Bead will now be sitting in front of slipped stitch
g	grams		
in	inch		
inc	increase		
k	knit		
k2tog	knit two stitches together.	psso	pass slipped stitch over
k2togtbl	knit 2 stitches together through the back of the loop	p2tog	purl two stitches together
		rep	repeat
k3tog	knit three stitches together	RS	right side of work
mb	make bobble: using yarn B, (k1, p1) twice into next st, (turn, p4, turn, k4) twice, turn, p4, turn and sl2, k2tog, psso	sl	slip
		st st	stocking stitch
		st/sts	stitch/stitches
		WS	wrong side of work
mm	millimetre	yb	yarn back
m1	make one stitch	yfwd	yarn forward
ML	make loop as follows: Knit into next stitch and before slipping the stitch off the left needle, bring yarn to the front of the	k	repeat instructions between k as many times as instructed
		( )	repeat instructions between ( ) as many times as instructed.

holding the yarn and needles

Before casting on it is a good idea to get used to holding the yarn and needles.
Remember, they are bound to feel really awkward at first.

Holding the needles

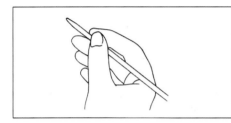

1 The right needle is held in the same way as a pencil (English). When casting on and working the first few rows the knitted piece passes over the hand, between the thumb and the index finger. As the work progresses, let the thumb slide under the knitted piece and hold the needle from below.

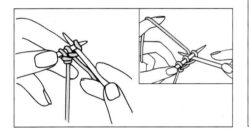

2 The left needle is held lightly over the top. If using the English method of knitting (main picture), the thumb and index finger control the tip of the needle. If using the Continental method (see inset,) control the tip with the thumb and middle finger.

Holding the yarn

There are several ways of winding the yarn around your fingers to control the tension; here are two of the simplest.

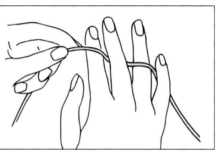

Method one
To hold the yarn in your right hand, pass it under your little finger, over your third finger, under your center finger and over your index finger. Your index finger is used to pass the yarn around the tip of the needle. The tension on the yarn is controlled by gripping the yarn in the crook of the little finger.

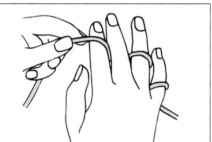

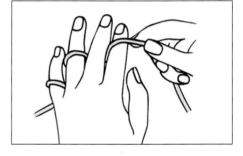

Method two
To hold the yarn in your right hand (left hand if using the Continental method, see inset), pass it under your little finger, then around this finger, over your third finger, under your center finger and over your index finger. Your index finger is used to pass the yarn around the tip of the needle. The yarn circled around your little finger creates the necessary tension for even knitting.

making a slip knot

A slip knot is the basis of all casting on techniques (see page 14) and is therefore the starting point for almost everything you do in knitting.

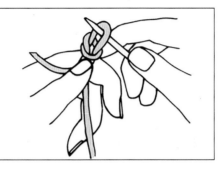

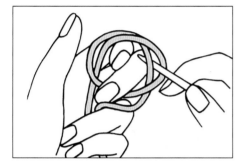

1 Wind the yarn around two fingers twice as shown. Insert a knitting needle through the first (front) strand and under the second (back) one.

2 Using the needle, pull the back strand through the front one to form a loop.

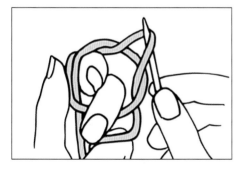

3 Holding the loose ends of the yarn with your left hand, pull the needle upwards, thus tightening the knot. Pull the ball end of the yarn again to tighten the knot further.

tips

Getting started

The yarn may be held in either the right or left hand; the two ways are referred to as the English and the Continental methods. Try holding the yarn in either of the ways shown opposite, though you may well develop a personal method. Ideally, ask a knitter to cast on a few stitches for you as it is easier to handle the yarn and needles with some stitches already cast on.

I usually use the cable method of casting on (see page 15). The cable method of casting on gives a firm, neat finish and is ideal for ribs.

If you knit very tightly you may need to use a larger needle size to cast on with.

casting on

Casting on is the term used for making a row of stitches to be used as a foundation for your knitting. There are several methods of casting on which produce different kinds of edges, but here are two examples, the cable method being my preferred option.

Thumb method

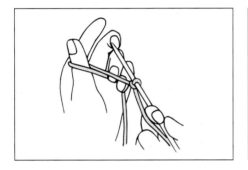

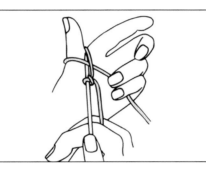

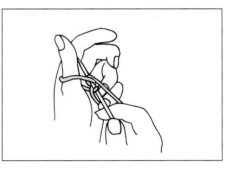

1 Make a slip knot 100 cm (40 in) from the end of the yarn. Hold the needle in your right hand with the ball end of the yarn over your index finger. *Wind the loose end of the yarn around your left thumb from front to back.

2 Insert the point of the needle under the first strand of yarn on your thumb.

3 With your right index finger, take the ball end of the yarn over the point of the needle.

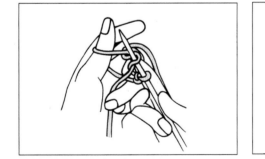

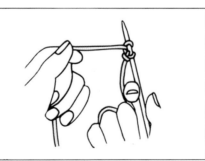

4 Pull a loop through to form the first stitch. Remove your left thumb from the yarn. Pull the loose end to secure the stitch (see inset). Repeat from * until the required number of stitches have been cast on.

Cable method

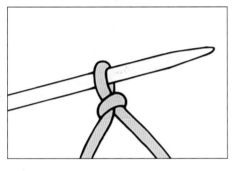

1 This method of casting on requires two needles. Make a slip knot about 10 cm (4 in) from the end of the yarn. Hold this needle in your left hand.

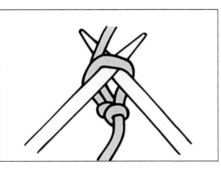

2 Insert the right-hand needle through the slip knot. Wrap the yarn over the point of the right-hand needle.

3 Pull a loop through the slip knot with the right-hand needle.

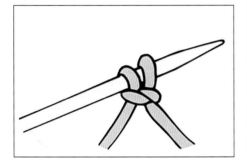

4 Place this loop on the left-hand needle. Gently pull the yarn to secure the stitch.

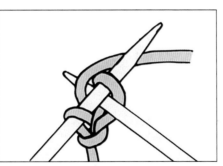

5 Insert the right-hand needle between the slip knot and the first stitch on the left-hand needle. Wrap the yarn round the point of the right-hand needle.

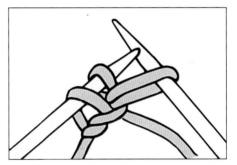

6 Draw a loop through, place this loop on the left-hand needle. Repeat steps 5 and 6 until the required number of stitches have been cast on.

the basic stitches

The knit and purl stitches form the basis of all knitted fabrics. The knit stitch is the easiest to learn and once you have mastered this you can move on to the purl stitch, which is the reverse of the knit stitch.

Knit stitch

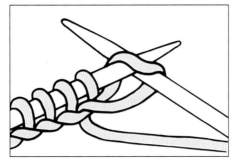

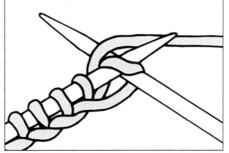

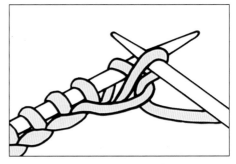

1 Hold the needle with the cast-on stitches in your left hand, with the loose yarn at the back of the work. Insert the right-hand needle from left to right through the front of the first stitch on the left-hand needle.

2 Wrap the yarn from left to right over the point of the right-hand needle.

3 Draw the yarn through the stitch, thus forming a new stitch on the right-hand needle.

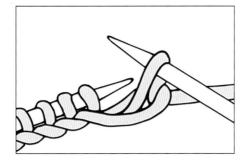

5 To knit a row, repeat steps 1 to 4 until all the stitches have been transferred from the left-hand needle to the right-hand needle. Turn the work, transferring the needle with the stitches to your left hand to work the next row.

4 Slip the original stitch off the left-hand needle, keeping the new stitch on the right-hand needle.

Purl stitch

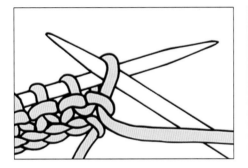

1 Hold the needle with the stitches in your left hand, with the loose yarn at the front of the work. Insert the right-hand needle from right to left into the front of the first stitch on the left-hand needle.

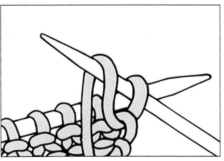

2 Wrap the yarn from right to left, up and over the point of the right-hand needle.

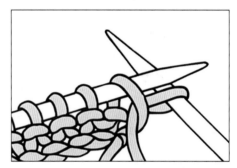

3 Draw the yarn through the stitch, thus forming a new stitch on the right-hand needle.

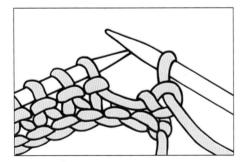

4 Slip the original stitch off the left-hand needle, keeping the new stitch on the right-hand needle.

5 To purl a row, repeat steps 1 to 4 until all the stitches have been transferred from the left-hand needle to the right-hand needle. Turn the work, transferring the needle with the stitches to your left hand to work the next row.

intarsia stitches

Intarsia is the name given to colour knitting where the pattern is worked in large blocks of colour at a time, requiring a separate ball of yarn for each area of colour as the yarn must not be stranded at the back.

Diagonal colour change with a slant to the left

This diagram shows a colour change on the wrong side of the work.

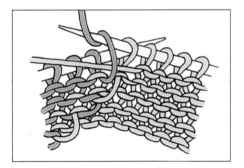

Use separate balls of yarn for each block of colour. On a right side row, with the yarns at the back of the work, the crossing of colours at joins happens automatically because of the encroaching nature of the pattern. On a wrong side row, with the yarns at the front of the work, take the first colour over the second colour, drop it then pick up the second colour underneath the first colour thus crossing the two colours together.

Diagonal colour change with a slant to the right

This diagram shows a colour change on the right side of the work.

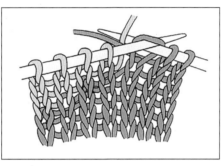

Use separate balls of yarn for each block of colour. On a right side row, with the yarns at the back of the work, take the first colour over the second colour, drop it then pick up the second colour underneath the first colour thus crossing the two colours over. On a wrong side row, with the yarns at the front of the work, the crossing of the two colours at the joins happens automatically because of the encroaching nature of the pattern.

Vertical colour change

This diagram shows a colour change on the wrong side of the work.

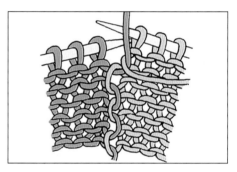

Use separate balls of yarn for each block of colour. Work in the first colour to the colour change, then drop the first colour, pick up the second colour underneath the first colour, crossing the two colours over before working the next stitch in the second colour. The first stitch after a colour change is worked firmly to avoid a gap forming between colours. This technique ensures that the yarns are crossed on every row and gives a neat vertical line between colours on the right side, and a vertical line of loops in each colour on the wrong side.

fair isle stitches

Stranding is used when the yarn not in use is left at the back of the work until needed. The loops formed by stranding are called 'floats' and it is important to ensure that they are not pulled too tightly when working the next stitch as this will pull in your knitting.

Stranding

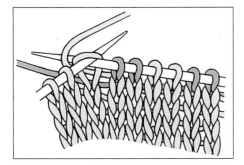

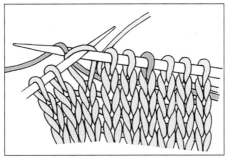

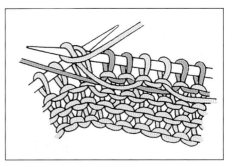

1 On a knit row, hold the first colour in your right hand and the second colour in your left hand. Knit the required number of stitches as usual with the first colour, carrying the second colour loosely across the wrong side of the work.

2 To knit a stitch in the second colour, insert the right-hand needle into the next stitch then draw a loop through from the yarn held in the left hand, carrying the yarn in the right hand loosely across the wrong side until required.

3 On a purl row, hold the yarns as for the knit rows. Purl the required number of stitches as usual with the first colour, carrying the second colour loosely across these stitches on the wrong side of the work.

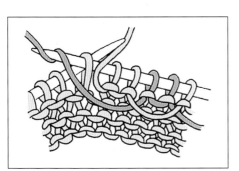

4 To purl a stitch in the second colour, insert the right-hand needle into the next stitch then draw a loop through from the yarn held in the left hand, carrying the yarn in the right hand loosely across the wrong side until next required.

increasing and decreasing

Many projects will require some shaping, either just to add interest or to allow them to fit comfortably. Shaping is achieved by increasing or decreasing the number of stiches you are working.

Increasing

The simplest method of increasing one stitch is to work into the front and back of the same stitch.

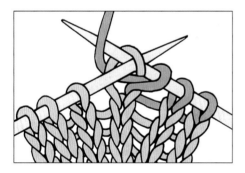

On a knit row, knit into the front of the stitch to be increased into, then before slipping it off the needle, place the right-hand needle behind the left-hand one and knit again into the back of it (inc). Slip the original stitch off the left-hand needle.

On a purl row, purl into the front of the stitch to be increased into, then before slipping it off the needle, purl again into the back of it. Slip the original stitch off the left-hand needle.

Decreasing

The simplest method of decreasing one stitch is to work two stitches together.

On a knit row, insert the right-hand needle from left to right through two stitches instead of one, then knit them together as one stitch. This is called knit two together (K2tog).

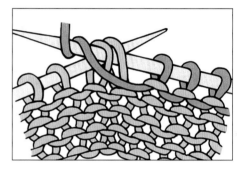

On a purl row, insert the right-hand needle from right to left through two stitches instead of one, then purl them together as one stitch. This is called purl two together (P2tog).

binding off

This is the most commonly-used method of securing stitches once you have finished a piece of knitting. The bound-off edge should have the same "give" or elasticity as the fabric and you should bind off in the stitch used for the main fabric unless the pattern directs otherwise.

Knitwise

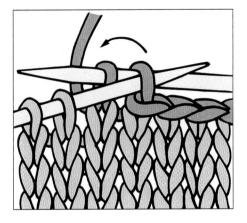

Knit two stitches. *Using the point of the left-hand needle lift the first stitch on the right-hand needle over the second then drop it off the needle. Knit the next stitch and repeat from * until all stitches have been worked off the left-hand needle and only one stitch remains on the right-hand needle. Cut the yarn, leaving enough to sew in the end, thread the end through the stitch then slip it off the needle. Draw the yarn up firmly to fasten off.

Purlwise

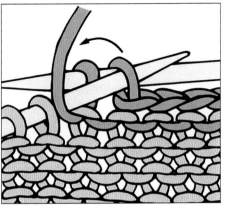

Purl two stitches. *Using the point of the left-hand needle lift the first stitch on the right-hand needle over the second and drop it off the needle. Purl the next stitch and repeat from * until all the stitches have been worked off the left-hand needle and only one stitch remains on the right-hand needle. Secure the last stitch as described in binding off knitwise.

tips

Binding off
The excitement of arriving at the last stage of your knitting can make you bind off without taking the same care that you have used in the rest of the work.

You should take into account the part of the project you are working on. If you are a tight knitter you may need to bind off with a larger needle, or if you are a loose knitter bind off with a smaller needle.

Lace stitches should also be bound off in pattern, slipping, making stitches, or decreasing as you go, to make sure that the fabric doesn't widen or gather up.

project index

Here's a gallery of all the specially designed projects featured in the book. They use a range of interesting new yarns to help create a truly unique look. Once you have become familiar with the basic techniques, you'll find all these projects easy and fun to make.

Floral   24

Angel   27

Mango   30

Violet   32

Ballerina   34

Mulberry   36

Spearmint   38

Fizz   40

Tutu   42

Swell   44

Berry   46

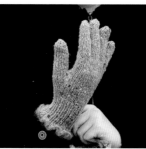

Fuchsia   48

Sage   50

Handy   53

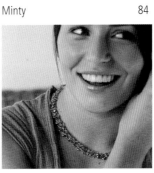

floral

Worked in a simple A-line shape, this ultra feminine bag is deceptively easy to knit.
Super cotton and nubby tweed create plenty of texture, and vibrant floral accents add
a dash of whimsy.

Materials

Yarn A Two 50g balls of Rowan Handknit Cotton,
Colour 219 Gooseberry

Yarn B Two 50g balls of Rowan Yorkshire Tweed
DK, Colour 348 Lime Leaf

Yarn C One 50g ball of Rowan All Seasons Cotton,
Colour 216 Citron

4 mm (US 6) needles

6 mm (US 10) needles

Lining fabric, approx. 60 × 60 cm
(24 × 24 in)

One small press stud (optional)

Gauge

14 sts and 20 rows to 10 cm (4 in) using one
strand of A and one strand of B on 6 mm (US 10)
needles measured over stocking stitch.

Finished size: 26.5 × 20 cm (10½ × 8 in)

Front and Back (make 1 of each)

Cast on 37 sts using one strand of A and one
strand of B held together on 6 mm (US 10)
needles.

Row 1: (RS) Knit.

Row 2: (WS) Purl.

Repeat last 2 rows once more, ending with a WS
row.

Row 5: K2tog, knit to last 2 sts, K2tog. (35 sts)

Row 6: Purl.

Row 7: Knit.

Row 8: Purl.

Row 9: Knit.

Row 10: Purl.

Row 11: K2tog, knit to last 2 sts, K2tog. (33 sts)

Repeat rows 6–11 four more times, ending with a
RS row. (25 sts)

Next: Purl.

Next: Knit.

Repeat last 2 rows once more, ending with a
RS row.

Next: Knit. (This creates garter stitch ridge for turn
over at top of bag.)

Next: Knit.

Next: Purl.
Repeat last 2 rows once more, ending with a
  WS row.
Cast off.

Handle

Cast on 5 sts using one strand of A and one strand
  of B held together on 6 mm (US 10) needles.
Row 1: (RS) Knit.
Row 2: (WS) K1, P3, K1.
Repeat last 2 rows until handle measures 32 cm
  (13 in) from cast-on edge, ending with a WS row.
Cast off.

Flowers (make 5)

Make two flowers using A, two using C, and one
using B as follows:
Cast on 93 sts using 4 mm (US 6) needles.
Row 1: K1, *K2, lift first of these sts over second,
  rep from * to end. (47 sts)
Row 2: P1, (P2tog) to end. (24 sts)
Row 3: Knit.
Row 4: Purl.

Break off yarn, thread through remaining sts and
pull together. Twist frill round into a flower shape
and secure using the yarn still attached.

Making up

Using the mattress stitch, sew together the front
and back of the bag by working down one side,
across the bottom and up the other side.

Make fabric lining as follows:
Using the knitted bag as a template, cut two pieces
of lining fabric slightly larger than the knitted
pieces plus 1 cm (^{3}/$_8$ in) at the sides and the bottom
for the seam allowance. Sew the two pieces
together by stitching down one side, across the
bottom and up the other side. Turn the knitted bag
inside out and with the lining fabric also inside out,
sew the bottom two corners of the lining to the
bottom two corners of the knitted bag. Keeping the
bag inside out, turn the lining back over the bag –
it will look as if the whole bag has been turned
inside out. Slip stitch the hems at the top of the
bag into place, at the same time securing and
covering the top edges of the lining. Turn the bag
the right side out.

Sew handle into place inside the bag at the top of
side seams and sew a press stud fastening into
place at top centre of the bag if desired. Sew
flowers into place using the photograph as a guide.

angel

This modern, everyday handbag is created using some simple shaping and is accentuated with garter-stitch ridges. The delicate texture of the flower and leaves offer a pretty contrast.

Materials

Yarn A Three 50g balls of Rowan All Seasons Cotton, Colour 192 Iceberg

Yarn B One 50g ball of Rowan 4 ply Soft, Colour 377 Wink

Yarn C One 25g ball of Rowan Kidsilk Haze, Colour 583 Blushes (used double)

Yarn D One 50g ball of Rowan Yorkshire Tweed DK, Colour 349 Frog

3.25 mm (US 3) needles

4.5 mm (US 7) needles

Lining fabric, approx. 80 × 80 cm (32 × 32 in)

One small press stud (optional)

Stitch marker

Gauge

18 sts and 25 rows to 10 cm (4 in) on 4.5 mm (US 7) needles measured over stocking stitch.

Finished size: 41.5 cm (16½ in) measured around

Front and Back (make 1 of each)

Cast on 45 sts using A and 4.5 mm (US 7) needles.

Row 1: (RS) Knit.

Row 2: (WS) Purl.

Row 3: Knit.

Repeat last 2 rows twice more, ending with a RS row.

Row 8: Knit. (This creates garter stitch ridge for turn over at top of bag.)

Row 9: Knit.

Row 10: Purl.

Repeat last 2 rows three more times, ending with a WS row.

Place markers on the 5th, 14th, 23rd, 32nd and 41st sts. You should have five marked sts in total.

Row 17: (inc row) K4, M1, knit marked st, M1 (K8, M1, knit marked st, M1) to last 4 sts, K4. (55 sts)

Row 18: Purl.

Row 19: Knit.

Repeat last row three more times, ending with a WS row.

Row 23: (inc row) K5, M1, knit marked st, M1 (K10, M1, knit marked st, M1) to last 5 sts, K5. (65 sts)

Row 24: Knit.

Repeat last row four more times, ending with a WS row.

Row 29: (inc row) K6, M1, knit marked st, M1 (K12, M1, knit marked st, M1) to last 6 sts, K6. (75 sts)

Row 30: Knit.

Repeat last row four more times, ending with a WS row.

Row 35: (dec row) K5, K2tog, knit marked st, K2tog (K10, K2tog, knit marked st, K2tog) to last 5 sts, K5. (65 sts)

Row 36: Knit.

Repeat last row four more times, ending with a WS row.

Row 41: (dec row) K4, K2tog, knit marked st, K2tog (K8, K2tog, knit marked st, K2tog) to last 4 sts, K4. (55 sts)

Row 42: Knit.

Repeat last row four more times, ending with a WS row.

Row 47: (dec row) K3, K2tog, knit marked st, K2tog (K6, K2tog, knit marked st, K2tog) to last 3 sts, K3. (45 sts)

Row 48: Knit.

Repeat last row twice more, ending with a WS row.

Row 51: (dec row) K2, K2tog, knit marked st, K2tog (K4, K2tog, knit marked st, K2tog) to last 2 sts, K2. (35 sts)

Row 52: Knit.

Cast off.

Handle (make 2)

Cast on 7 sts, using A and 4.5 mm (US 7) needles.

Row 1: (RS) Knit.

Row 2: (WS) K1, P5, K1.

Repeat last 2 rows until work measures 35 cm (14 in) from cast-on edge, ending with a WS row.

Cast off.

Flowers (make 3)

Cast on 73 sts using C and 3.25 mm (US 3) needles.

Change to B.

Row 1: K1 *K2, lift first of these sts over second, rep from * to end. (37 sts)

Row 2: P1, (P2tog) to end. (19 sts)

Break off yarn, thread through remaining stitches and pull together. Twist frill around into a flower shape and secure, using the yarn still attached.

Leaves (make 4)

Cast on 3 sts using D and 3.25 mm (US 3) needles.

Row 1: K1, P1, K1.

Row 2: K1, M1, K1, M1, K1. (5 sts)

Row 3: K1, P3, K1.

Row 4: K2, M1, K1, M1, K2. (7 sts)

Row 5: K1, P5, K1.

Row 6: K3, M1, K1, M1, K3. (9 sts)

Row 7: K1, P7, K1.

Row 8: K3, sl2, K1, p2sso, K3. (7 sts)

Row 9: K1, P5, K1.

Row 10: K2, sl2, K1, p2sso, K2. (5 sts)

Row 11: K1, P3, K1.

Row 12: K1, sl2, K1, p2sso, K1. (3 sts)

Row 13: K1, P1, K1.

Row 14: Sl2, K1, p2sso. (1 st)

Fasten off.

Making up

Using the mattress stitch, sew the font and back of the bag together by working down one side, across the bottom and up the other side.

Make fabric lining as follows:

> **note**
>
> As this is a shaped bag, the pieces of fabric lining need to be considerably larger than the knitted pieces so that the lining can 'fill out' inside the bag.

Using the knitted bag as a template, cut two pieces of lining fabric larger than the knitted pieces plus 1 cm (3/8 in) at the sides and the bottom for the seam allowance. Sew the two pieces together by working down one side, across the bottom and up the other side. Turn the knitted bag inside out and with the lining fabric also inside out, sew the bottom two corners of the lining to the bottom two corners of the knitted bag. Keeping the knitted bag inside out, turn the lining back over the bag – it will look as if the whole bag has been turned inside out. Slip stitch hems at the top of the bag in place, at the same time securing and covering the top edges of the lining. Turn the bag right side out.

Sew a press stud fastening into place at top centre of the bag if desired.

Sew flowers and leaves into place using photograph as a guide.

Sew the handles to the top of the bag, 3 cm (1 1/4 in) in from each side seam.

mango

Style and practicality team up to make this easy-going tote an ideal everyday carry-all. Oversized cables and bobbles knit in chunky yarn lend maximum textural interest, while an eye-popping palette gives it a contemporary edge.

Materials

Yarn A Two 100g balls of Rowan Big Wool, Colour 029 Pistachio

Yarn B Two 100g balls of Rowan Ribbon Twist, Colour 111 Ribble

12 mm (US 17) needles

Cable needle

Lining fabric, approx. 80 × 80 cm (32 × 32 in)

One large press stud (optional)

Gauge

10 sts and 11 rows to 10 cm (4 in) on 12 mm (US 17) needles measured over cable pattern.

Finished size: 32 × 30 cm (13 × 12 in)

Abbreviations

MB Make Bobble: Using B, knit into the front, back and front of next st (3 sts), turn P3, turn K3, turn p3, turn sl 1, K2tog, psso.

C4B Cable 4 Back: Slip next 2 sts onto cable needle and hold at back of work, K2 sts from left-hand needle, then K2 sts from cable needle.

Front

Cast on 32 sts with A and 12 mm (US 17) needles.

Row 1: (RS) P5 (K4, P5) to end.

Row 2: (WS) K5 (P4, K5) to end.

Repeat last 2 rows once more ending with a WS row.

Row 5: P2, MB, P2, (K4, P2, MB, P2) to end.

Row 6: Work as row 2.

Row 7: P5, (C4B, P5) to end.

Row 8: Work as row 2.

Row 9: Work as row 1.

Row 10: Work as row 2.

Rep rows 5–10 three more times and then repeat rows 5–8 again, ending with a WS row.

Next: Purl. (This creates garter st ridge for turn over at top of bag.)

Change to B.

Next: Purl.

Next: Knit.

Next: Purl.

Cast off.

Back

Work as for the front, omitting bobbles.

Base

Cast on 8 sts with B and 12 mm (US 17) needles.

Row 1: (RS) Knit.

Row 2: (WS) Purl.

Repeat last 2 rows until work measures 32 cm (13 in) from cast-on edge, ending with a WS row (or until base will fit neatly along the cast-on edges of the front and back).

Cast off.

Sides and handle (knitted in one piece)

Cast on 8 sts with B and 12 mm (US 17) needles.

Row 1: (RS) Knit.

Row 2: (WS) K1, P6, K1.

Repeat last 2 rows until work measures 105 cm (42 in) from cast-on edge, ending with a WS row.

Cast off.

Making up

Using the mattress stitch, sew the side edges of the base to the cast-on edges of the front and back. Sew the cast-on edge of the side/handle to the left hand end of the base, and the bound-off edge to the right-hand end of the base.

Make fabric lining as follows:

Using the knitted bag as a template, cut two pieces of fabric slightly larger than the front and back, plus 1 cm (³⁄₈ in) at sides and bottom for seams. Do the same for the base and two sides, allowing 1 cm (³⁄₈ in) all around. Make a 1 cm (³⁄₈ in) seam across the top of the two side pieces, as they will be seen. Sew the lining together as for the knitted pieces. Turn the bag inside out, and with the lining also inside out, sew the bottom four corners of the lining to the bottom four corners of the bag. Turn the lining back over the bag. Slip stitch the lining at the top of the bag into place, covering the top edges of the lining. Turn the bag right side out.

Sew a press stud fastening inside the top centre of the bag.

violet

A shapely little evening purse with glittering bead detail is perfect for a night on the town. Knitting with beads is a great way of adding a hint of sophistication and glamour. Once you have seen how simple it is to do, you'll be applying beads to everything!

Materials

One 50g ball of Rowan Cotton Glace,
  Colour 787 Hyacinth
3.25 mm (US 3) needles
Approx. 143 purple beads, 3 mm (J3001014)

Gauge

23 sts and 32 rows to 10 cm (4 in) on 3.25 mm (US 3) needles measured over stocking stitch.

Finished size: 17 (widest point at top) × 18 cm (6¾ × 7¼ in)

Abbreviation

PB Place Bead: WYIF, slip bead to front of work, sl 1 purlwise, take yarn to back of work. The bead will now be sitting in front of the slipped stitch (see page 80).

Front

Cast on 39 sts using 3.25 mm (US 3) needles.
Row 1: (RS) Knit.
This row forms garter stitch. Repeat this row 11 more times, ending with a WS row.
Row 13: Knit.
Row 14: Purl.
Row 15: (eyelet row) K4 (YO, K2tog, K4) to last 5 sts, YO, K2tog, K3.
Row 16: Purl.
Row 17: Knit.
Row 18: Purl.*

Row 19: K1, PB, (K5, PB) to last st, K1.
Row 20: Purl.
Row 21: Knit.
Row 22: Purl.
Row 23: K4, PB, (K5, PB) to last 4 sts, K4.
Row 24: Purl.
Row 25: Knit.
Row 26: Purl.
Rows 19–26 form the pattern. Repeat these rows 4 more times and then repeat row 19 once more, ending with a RS row.
**Next: Purl.
Next: K2, sl 1, K1, psso (k3, sl 1, K1, psso) to last 5 sts, K2, sl 1, K1, psso, K1. (31 sts)
Next: Purl.
Next: K2, sl 1, K1, psso (K2, sl 1, K1, psso) to last 3 sts, K3. (24 sts)
Next: Purl.
Next: K2, sl 1, K1, psso (K1, sl 1, K1, psso) to last 2 sts, K2. (17 sts)
Next: Purl.
Next: K1, (sl 1, K1, psso) to end. (9 sts)
Next: Purl.
Next: K1 (sl 1, K1, psso) to end. (5 sts)
Do not cast off. Break off yarn and thread through remaining sts and pull together.

Back

Work as for front until * and then as follows:
Row 19: K4, PB (K5, PB) to last 4 sts, K4.
Row 20: Purl.

Row 21: Knit.
Row 22: Purl.
Row 23: K1, PB (K5, PB) to last st, K1.
Row 24: Purl.
Row 25: Knit.
Row 26: Purl.
Rows 19–26 form the pattern. Repeat these rows 4 more times and then repeat row 19 once more, ending with a RS row.
Now work as for front from ** to end.

Handle

Make a twisted cord as follows: Cut 2 lengths of yarn approx. 125 cm (50 in) long and knot them together at each end. Ask someone to hold one end of the yarn while you hold the other. With the yarn stretched out, twist the ends in opposite directions until the cord begins to twist back on itself. Bring the two ends together and hold tightly, allowing the two halves to twist together. Smooth out any bumps by running your fingers up and down the cord. You now have a twisted cord approximately 50 cm (20 in) long. Knot ends and smooth.

Making up

Using the mattress stitch, sew the front and back of the bag together by working down one side, around the bottom and up the other side.

Thread the twisted cord through the eyelets, bringing ends out to tie.

ballerina

The fuzzy, ruffled edge offers a softness and balance to the textured rib of this elongated handbag. A knotted handle is an unusual, yet simple, addition.

Materials

Yarn A One 25g ball of Rowan Kidsilk Haze, Colour 583 Blushes (used double)

Yarn B One 50g ball of Rowan Yorkshire Tweed DK, Colour 350 Frolic

4 mm (US 6) needles

Lining fabric approx. 36 × 50 cm (14 × 20 in)

One small press stud (optional)

Gauge

21 sts and 30 rows to 10 cm (4 in) on 4 mm (US 6) needles measured over pattern.

Finished size: 14.75 × 22 cm (5⅞ × 8¾ in)

Front and Back (make 1 of each)

Cast on 121 sts using A and 4 mm (US 6) needles.

Row 1: (RS) K1, (K2, lift first of these over second) to end. (61 sts)

Row 2: (WS) P1, (P2tog) to end. (31 sts)

Row 3: Knit.

Row 4: Purl.

Change to B.

Row 5: Knit.

Row 6: (K1, P1) to last st, K1.

Repeat last 2 rows until work measures 22 cm (8¾ in) from beginning of row 5, ending with a WS row.

Cast off.

Handle (make 2)

Cast on 5 sts using B and 4 mm (US 6) needles.

Row 1: (RS) Knit.

Row 2: (WS) K1, P3, K1.

Repeat last 2 rows until handle measures 30 cm (12 in) from cast-on edge, ending with a WS row. Cast off.

Making up

Using the mattress stitch, sew the front and back of the bag together by working down one side, across the bottom and up the other side. Sew the bound-off edge of one of the handles to the inside of the bag, at the top of the left side seam. Then sew the bound-off edge of the other handle to the inside of the bag at the top of the right side seam.

Make fabric lining as follows:

Using the knitted bag as a template, cut out two pieces of lining fabric slightly larger than the knitted pieces plus 1 cm (⅜ in) all the way around for the seam allowance. Sew a 1 cm (⅜ in) hem across the top edges of both pieces to neaten them up, since they will be seen. Sew the two pieces together by working down one side, across the bottom and up the other side.

Turn the knitted bag inside out. With the lining fabric also inside out, sew the bottom two corners of the lining to the bottom two corners of the knitted bag. Keeping the knitted bag inside out, turn the fabric lining back over the bag. It will now look as if the whole bag has been turned inside out. Slip stitch the lining into place around the top of the bag. Turn the bag the right way out.

Sew a press stud in place at the top centre of bag, if desired. Tie the two cast-on edges of the handles together with a knot.

mulberry

Mohair and tweed work together to create a very soft knit in this satchel-style bag. A garter-stitch 'belt' with buckle fastening makes a quirky addition.

Materials

Yarn A Two 50g balls of Rowan Felted Tweed, Colour 151 Bilberry

Yarn B Two 50g balls of Rowan Kid Classic, Colour 835 Royal

5 mm (US 8) needles

4 mm (US 6) needles

One purple buckle (Rowan 00361), 4 x 6 cm (1 ½ x 2 ¼ in)

Lining fabric, approx. 60 × 60 cm (24 × 24 in)

One small press stud (optional)

Gauge

17 sts and 24 rows to 10 cm (4 in) using one strand of A and one strand of B and 5 mm (US 8) needles measured over stocking stitch.

Finished size: 26.5 × 23 cm (10½ × 9¼ in)

Front and Back (make one of each)

Cast on 45 sts using one strand of A and one strand of B and 5 mm (US 8) needles.

Row 1: (RS) Knit.

Row 2: (WS) Purl.

Repeat last 2 rows until work measures 23 cm (9¼ in) from cast-on edge, ending with a RS row.

Next: Knit. (This creates garter st ridge for turn over at top of bag.)

Next: Knit.

Next: Purl.

Repeat last 2 rows once more, ending with a WS row.

Cast off.

Sides, base and handle (knitted all in one piece)

Cast on 7 sts using B and 4 mm (US 6) needles.

Row 1: (RS) Knit.

Repeat this row until work measures 120 cm (48 in) from cast-on edge, ending with WS row.

Cast off.

Belt

Cast on 13 sts using B and 4 mm (US 6) needles.

Row 1: (RS) Knit.

Repeat this row until work measures 64 cm (25 ½ in) from cast-on edge, ending with WS row.

Cast off.

Making up

Join the cast-on edge of the sides/base/handle to the bound-off edge. With the join at the centre of the base, use mattress stitch to sew the base section of the sides/base/handle to the cast-on edges of the front and back of the bag. Sew the rest of the sides/handle into position.

Make fabric lining as follows:

Using the knitted bag as a template, cut out two pieces of lining fabric slightly larger than the front and back pieces, plus 1 cm (3/8 in) seam allowance at the side and bottom edges. Do the same for the base and two sides, but allowing 1 cm (3/8 in) for the seam all the way around. The two pieces of fabric that are to line the sides must be given a 1 cm (3/8 in) seam across the top to neaten them up as they will be seen. Sew the lining together as you did for the knitted pieces. Turn the knitted bag inside out and with the lining fabric also inside out, sew the bottom four corners of the lining to the bottom four corners of the knitted bag. Keeping the knitted bag inside out, turn the fabric lining back over the bag. It will now look as if the whole bag has been turned inside out. Slip stitch the knitted hems at the top of the bag into place, securing and covering the top edges of the lining. Turn the bag the right side out.

Sew a press stud into place at the top centre of the bag if desired.

Thread the bound-off edge of the belt around the middle post of the buckle and slip stitch into place. Now the buckle is attached to the belt, position and fasten belt around the bag using the photograph as a guide. Slip stitch belt into place neatly and securely.

spearmint

This spirited zigzag scarf achieves its striking geometric shape with basic increasing and decreasing. Stripes of mohair and Lurex Shimmer are echoed in the long tassels at the ends.

Materials

Yarn A Two 50g balls of Rowan Yorkshire Tweed DK, Colour 347 Skip

Yarn B One 25g ball of Rowan Kidsilk Haze, Colour 582 Trance

Yarn C One 25g ball of Rowan Lurex Shimmer, Colour 333 Pewter

4 mm (US 6) needles

Large crochet hook

Gauge

22 sts and 30 rows to 10 cm (4 in) on 4 mm (US 6) needles measured over stocking stitch.

Finished size: 12.5 × 150 cm (5 × 60 in)

Scarf

Cast on 1 st using A and 4 mm (US 6) needles.

Row 1: (RS) Increase into st. (2 sts)

Row 2: (WS) Increase into first st, K1. (3 sts)

Row 3: Knit.

Row 4: Knit.

Row 5: K1, M1, knit to last st, M1, K1. (5 sts)

Repeat last 2 rows until 27 sts, ending with a RS row.

Next: Knit.

Next: K1, K2togtbl, knit to last 3 sts, K2tog, K1. (25 sts)

Next: Knit.

Repeat last 2 rows until 11 sts, ending with a WS row.

*Change to one strand of B and one strand of C.

Next: Knit.

Repeat last row 3 more times, ending with a WS row.

Change to A.

Next: Knit.

Next: Knit.

Next: K1, M1, knit to last st, M1, K1. (13 sts)

Repeat last 2 rows until 27 sts, ending with a RS row.

Next: Knit.

Next: K1, K2togtbl, knit to last 3 sts, K2tog, K1. (25 sts)

Next: Knit.

Repeat last 2 rows until 11 sts, ending with a WS row.

Repeat from * 10 more times, ending with a WS row.

Change to one strand of B and one strand of C.

Next: Knit.

Repeat last row 3 more times, ending with a WS row.

Change to A.

Next: Knit.

Next: Knit.

Next: K1, M1, knit to last st, M1, K1. (13 sts)

Repeat last 2 rows until 27 sts, ending with a RS row.

Next: Knit.

Next: K1, K2togtbl, knit to last 3 sts, K2tog, K1. (25 sts)

Next: Knit.

Repeat last 2 rows until 5 . ending with a WS row.

Next: K1, K3tog, K1. (3 sts)

Next: Knit.

Next: Sl 2, K1, p2sso.

Fasten off.

Tassels (make 2)

Cut 42 cm (17 in) lengths of yarn as follows: 2 lengths of A, 4 lengths of B and 2 lengths of C. Hold all 8 strands of yarn together and fold in half. Using a large crochet hook, thread the folded loop through the cast-on edge at the point of the first diamond, pull the ends through the loop and then pull them to secure the tassel. Make another tassel the same way and join at the bound-off edge at the point of the last diamond.

fizz

A bold ruffle and wide rib combine to create this eye-catching, short scarf. A narrow opening at one end allows you to tuck the other end of the scarf through for a snug fit.

Materials

Yarn A One 50g ball of Rowan Wool Cotton, Colour 958 Aloof (used double)

Yarn B Two 50g hanks of Rowan Summer Tweed, Colour 527 Sprig

5 mm (US 8) needles

2 stitch holders

Spare knitting needle

Gauge

16 sts and 23 rows to 10 cm (4 in) on 5 mm (US 8) needles measured over stocking stitch.

Finished size: 21.75 × 80 cm (8³⁄₄ × 32 in)

First panel

Cast on 137 sts using A (used double) and 5mm (US 8) needles.

Row 1: (RS) K1, (K2, lift first of these over second) to end. (69 sts)

Row 2: (WS) P1, (P2tog) to end. (35 sts)

Change to B.

Row 3: K4, P3, (K3, P3) to last 4 sts, K4.

Row 4: K1, P3, (K3, P3) to last st, K1.

Repeat last 2 rows 8 more times, ending with a WS row.

Divide for slit as follows:

Next row: K4, (P3, K3) twice, P1, K1, turn.

Next row: Bind off one st, then (P3, K3) twice, P3, K1. (17 sts, including st used to bind off)

Next row: K4, (P3, K3) twice, K1.

Next row: K1, (P3, K3) twice, P3, K1.

Repeat last 2 rows 10 more times, ending with a WS row.

Next row: K4, (P3, K3) twice, K1.

Leave these 17 sts on a holder. Break off yarn.

With RS facing, rejoin yarn to remaining 17 sts and work as follows:

Next row: (RS) K1, (K3, P3) twice, K4.

Next row: (WS) K1, (P3, K3) twice, P3, K1.

Repeat last 2 rows 11 more times, ending with a WS row.

Next row: K1, (K3, P3) twice, K4.

You will now have two sections of knitting. Join these two sections as follows:

Next row: K1 (P3, K3) twice, P3, K1, cast on 1 st, and then (working across the 17 sts on the holder), K1, (P3, K3) twice, P3, K1. (35 sts)

The two sections are now joined and you will have all 35 sts back onto one needle.

Continue as follows:

Next row: K4, P3, (K3, P3) to last 4 sts, K4.

Next row: K1, P3, (K3, P3) to last st, K1.

Repeat last 2 rows until scarf measures 40 cm (16 in) from cast-on edge, ending with a WS row.

Do not cast off. Leave sts on a holder.

Second panel

Cast on 137 sts using A (used double) and 5 mm (US 8) needles.

Row 1: (RS) K1, (K2, lift first of these sts over second) to end. (69 sts)

Row 2: (WS) P1, (P2tog) to end. (35 sts)

Change to B.

Row 3: K4, P3, (K3, P3) to last 4 sts, K4.

Row 4: K1, P3, (K3, P3) to last st, K1.

Repeat last 2 rows until scarf measures 40 cm (16 in) from cast-on edge, ending with a WS row.

Do not cast off. Leave sts on a holder.

Making up

Slip the first scarf panel onto one needle and the second scarf panel onto another needle. Hold the two panels together with right sides facing each other (wrong sides facing outward), and using a third needle, knit the first st on the front needle together with the first st on the back needle. Do the same for the second sts and then cast off by lifting 1 st over the other. Continue in this way until all sts have been bound off.

tutu

Frilly layers of contrasting textures are used to create this and easy-to-knit, ribbed scarf. Tackle one layer at a time and you'll have this sumptous neckwarmer stitched in no time at all!

Materials

Yarn A One 50g ball of Rowan Kid Classic, Colour 844 Frilly (used triple)

Yarn B One 100g ball of Rowan Chunky Print, Colour 074 Tart

Yarn C Two 100g balls of Rowan Plaid, Colour 164 Sea Thistle

8 mm (US 11) needles

Stitch holder

Spare knitting needle

Gauge

11 sts and 14 rows to 10 cm (4 in) on 8 mm (US 11) needles measured over stocking stitch.

Finished Size: 19 × 180 cm (7½ × 72 in)

Scarf panel (make 2)

First Section

Cast on 81 sts using A (used triple) and 8 mm (US 11) needles.

Row 1: (RS) K1, (K2, lift first of these sts over second) to end. (41 sts)

Row 2: (WS) P1 (P2tog) to end. (21 sts)

Row 3: Knit.

Row 4: K1, (P1, K1) to end.

Repeat last 2 rows 9 more times, ending with a WS row.

Do not cast off. Leave sts on a holder.

Second Section

Cast on 81 sts using B and 8 mm (US 11) needles.

Row 1: (RS) K1, (K2, lift first of these sts over second) to end. (41 sts)

Row 2: (WS) P1, (P2tog) to end. (21 sts)

Next row: Join the second section to the first section as follows: with RS facing, knit together the first st on the needle with the first st on the holder. Continue in this way until the whole row has been completed.

Next row: K1, (P1, K1) to end.

Next row: Knit.

Next row: K1, (P1, K1) to end.

Repeat last 2 rows eight more times, ending with a WS row.

Do not cast off. Leave sts on a holder.

Third Section

Cast on 81 sts using C and 8 mm (US 11) needles.

Row 1: (RS) K1, (K2, lift first of these sts over second) to end. (41 sts)

Row 2: (WS) P1, (P2tog) to end. (21 sts)

Next row: Join the third section to the second section as follows: with RS facing, knit together the first st on the needle with the first st on the holder. Continue in this way until the whole row has been completed.

Next row: K1 (P1, K1) to end.

Next row: Knit.

Next row: K1 (P1, K1) to end.

Repeat last 2 rows until work measures 90 cm (36 in) from cast-on edge, ending with a WS row.

Do not cast off. Leave sts on a holder.

Making up

Slip the first scarf panel onto one needle and the second scarf panel onto another needle. Hold the two panels together with right sides facing each other (wrong sides facing outward), and using a third needle, knit the first st on the front needle together with the first st on the back needle. Do the same for the second sts and then cast off by lifting one st over the other. Continue in this way until all sts have been bound off.

swell

Plain and tweed yarn come together to form this quick-stitch bobble hat. A wide ribbed band and a traditional pom-pom on the top finish it off nicely!

Materials

Yarn A One 50g ball of Rowan Wool Cotton, Colour 946 Elf

Yarn B One 50g ball of Rowan Felted Tweed, Colour 152 Watery

4 mm (US 6) needles

Two circles of cardboard approx. 3.5 cm (1³⁄₈ in) in diameter

Gauge

22 sts and 30 rows to 10 cm (4 in) on 4 mm (US 6) needles measured over stocking stitch.

Finished size: to fit average-size adult head

Hat

Cast on 104 sts using A and 4 mm (US 6) needles.

Change to B.

Row 1: (RS) K4, (P3, K3) to last 4 sts, P4.

Repeat this row 13 more times, ending with a WS row.

Change to A.

Next row: Knit, inc 2 sts evenly across this row. (106 sts)

Next row: Purl.

Next row: Knit.

**Change to B.

Next row: Knit.

Next row: Knit.

Next row: Purl.

Next row: Knit.

Change to A.

Next row: Knit.

Next row: Knit.

Next row: Purl.

Next row: Knit.

Repeat from ** twice more, ending with a RS row.

Change to B.

Next row: Knit.

Next row: Knit.

Next row: Purl.

Next row: Knit.

Change to A.

Next row: Knit.

Next row: Knit.

Next row: Purl.

Working in set stripe sequence, shape crown as follows:

Next row: (dec row) K1, (K2tog, K5) to end. (91 sts)

Next row: Knit.

Next row: (dec row) K1, (K2tog, K4) to end. (76 sts)

Next row: Purl.

Next row: (dec row) K1, (K2tog, K3) to end. (61 sts)

Next row: Knit.

Next row: (dec row) K1, (K2tog, K2) to end. (46 sts)

Next row: Purl.

Next row: (dec row) K1, (K2tog, K1) to end. (31 sts)

Next row: Knit.

Next row: (dec row) K1, (K2tog) to end. (16 sts)

Do not cast off.

Making up

Thread yarn through remaining sts and pull together. Sew seam starting at the crown and working to the cast-on edge.

Make pom-pom as follows:

Cut a hole in the centre of each circle of cardboard approx. 1.5 cm (⁵⁄₈ in) in diameter. Hold one strand of A and one strand of B together and wind the yarn through the hole and around the outside of the two circles of cardboard until the centre hole is almost filled. Next, cut slowly and carefully around the edges of the two pieces of cardboard until all the yarn has been cut. Carefully ease the pieces of cardboard apart but before taking them off completely, tie a piece of yarn in a secure knot around the center of the pom-pom to hold it together. Now remove the cardboard.

Sew pom-pom to crown of hat.

berry

This beanie style hat has pretty scalloped edging and bead detail. The rich flecks of colour in the tweed adds textural verve to this interesting design.

Materials

Yarn A One 50g ball of Rowan Handknit Cotton, Colour 314 Decadent

Yarn B One 50g ball of Rowan Yorkshire Tweed, Colour 342 Revel

4 mm (US 6) needles

Approx. 78 purple beads, 3 mm (J3001014)

Gauge

22 sts and 30 rows to 10 cm (4 in) on 4 mm (US 6) needles measured over stocking stitch.

Finished size: to fit average-size adult head.

Abbreviation

PB Place Bead: with yarn in front, slip bead to front of work, sl 1 purlwise, take yarn to back of work. The bead will now be sitting in front of the slipped stitch (see p.80).

Hat

Cast on 106 sts using B and 4 mm (US 6) needles. Change to A.

Row 1: (RS) K1, (sl 1, K1, psso, K9, K2tog) to last st, K1. (90 sts)

Row 2: (WS) Purl.

Row 3: K1, (sl 1, K1, psso, K7, K2tog) to last st, K1. (74 sts)

Row 4: Purl.

Row 5: K1, *sl 1, K1, psso, YO, [K1, YO] 5 times, K2tog, rep from * to last st, K1. (106 sts)

Row 6: Knit.

Repeat rows 1–6 once more, ending with a WS row. Change to B.

Row 13: Knit.

Row 14: Purl.

Change to A.

Row 15: Knit.

Row 16: Purl.

Row 17: K1, PB, (K3, PB) to last 4 sts, K4.

Row 18: Purl.

Row 19: (K3, PB) to last 2 sts, K2.

Row 20: Purl.

Row 21: K1, PB, (K3, PB) to last 4 sts, K4.

Row 22: Purl.

Change to B.

Continue in St st until hat measures 18 cm (7¼ in) from cast-on edge, ending with a WS row.

Next row: (dec row) K1, (K2tog, K5) to end. (91 sts)

Next row: Purl.

Next row: (dec row) K1, (K2tog, K4) to end. (76 sts)

Next row: Purl.

Next row: (dec row) K1, (K2tog, K3) to end. (61 sts)

Next row: Purl.

Next row: (dec row) K1, (K2tog, K2) to end. (46 sts)

Next row: Purl.

Next row: (dec row) K1, (K2tog, K1) to end. (31 sts)

Next row: Purl.

Next row: (dec row) K1, (K2tog) to end. (16 sts)

Do not cast off.

Making up

Thread yarn through remaining sts and pull together. Sew seam starting at the crown and working to the cast-on edge.

fuchsia

The simplest of beanies, this one can be knitted in next to no time. A single bloom adds a fun, youthful touch.

Materials

Yarn A One 50g ball of Rowan Wool Cotton, Colour 943 Flower

Yarn B Two 50g balls of Rowan 4 ply Soft, Colour 377 Wink (used double)

4 mm (US 6) needles

Gauge

22 sts and 30 rows to 10 cm (4 in) on 4 mm (US 6) needles measured over stocking stitch.

Finished size: to fit average-size adult head

Hat

Cast on 106 sts using A and 4 mm (US 6) needles. Change to B.

Row 1: (RS) (K1, P1) to end.

Row 2: (WS) (P1, K1) to end.

These 2 rows form seed st. Repeat these 2 rows 3 more times, ending with a WS row.

Change to A.

Next row: Knit.

Next row: Purl.

These last 2 rows form St st. Repeat last 2 rows once more.

Change to B.

Continue in St st until hat measures 18 cm (7¼ in) from cast-on edge, ending with a WS row.

Shape crown as follows:

Next row: (dec row) K1, (K2tog, K5) to end. (91 sts)

Next row: Purl.

Next row: (dec row) K1, (K2tog, K4) to end. (76 sts)

Next row: Purl.

Next row: (dec row) K1, (K2tog, K3) to end. (61 sts)

Next row: Purl.

Next row: (dec row) K1, (K2tog, K2) to end. (46 sts)

Next row: Purl.

Next row: (dec row) K1, (K2tog, K1) to end. (31 sts)

Next row: Purl.

Next row: (dec row) K1, (K2tog) to end. (16 sts)

Do not cast off. Thread yarn through remaining sts and pull together.

Flower

Cast on 93 sts using A and 4 mm (US 6) needles. Change to B.

Row 1: K1, (K2, lift first of these sts over second) to end. (47 sts)

Row 2: P1, (P2tog) to end. (24 sts)

Row 3: Knit.

Row 4: Purl.

Do not cast off. Thread yarn through remaining sts and pull together. Twist into flower shape and sew to secure.

Finishing

Sew seam starting at the crown and working to the cast-on edge. Sew flower into place using the photograph as a guide.

sage

Accessories can be both fun and practical. Flirty frills accent the cuff of these stylish gloves, and tweedy wool yarn will keep your hands toasty all winter long.

Materials

Yarn A One 50g ball of Rowan Felted Tweed, Colour 146 Herb

Yarn B One 25g ball of Rowan Kidsilk Haze, Colour 597 Jelly (used double)

Yarn C One 50g ball of Rowan Handknit Cotton, Colour 219 Gooseberry

3.25 mm (US 3) needles

4 mm (US 6) needles

Gauge

22 sts and 30 rows to 10 cm (4 in) on 4 mm (US 6) needles measured over stocking stitch.

Finished size: to fit average-size adult hand

Right Hand

Cast on 173 sts using B and 3.25 mm (US 3) needles.

Change to C.

Row 1: (RS) K1, (K2, lift first of these sts over second) to end. (87 sts)

Row 2: (WS) P1, (P2tog) to end. (44 sts)

Change to A.

Row 3: (K1, P1) to end.

Repeat this row 23 more times, ending with a WS row.

Change to 4 mm (US 6) needles.

Next row: (inc row) K7, M1, knit to last 7 sts, M1, K7. (46 sts)

Next row: Purl.

Next row: Knit.

Next row: Purl.

*Shape thumb as follows:

Next row: K23, M1, K3, M1, knit to end. (48 sts)

Next row: Purl.

Next row: K23, M1, K5, M1, knit to end. (50 sts)

Next row: Purl.

Next row: K23, M1, K7, M1, knit to end. (52 sts)

Next row: Purl.

Next row: K23, M1, K9, M1, knit to end. (54 sts)

Next row: Purl.

Next row: K23, M1, K11, M1, knit to end. (56 sts)

Next row: Purl.

Next row: K23, M1, K13, M1, knit to end. (58 sts)

Next row: Purl.

Divide for thumb as follows:

Next row: K38, turn.

Next row: P15, turn.

Starting with a knit row, work 14 rows of St st on these 15 sts only, ending with a WS row.

Next row: (K1, K2tog) to end. (10 sts)

Next row: Purl.

Next row: (K2tog) to end. (5 sts)

Break off yarn and thread through remaining 5 sts and pull together.

With RS facing, rejoin yarn at base of thumb to remaining sts and knit to end. (43 sts)

Next row: Purl.

Next row: Knit.

Next row: Purl.

Repeat last 2 rows 4 more times, ending with a WS row.

Work first finger as follows:

Next row: K28, turn.

Next row: P13, turn and cast on 2 sts. (15 sts)

Starting with a knit row, work 18 rows of St st on these 15 sts only, ending with a WS row.

Next row: (K1, K2tog) to end. (10 sts)

Next row: Purl.

Next row: (K2tog) to end. (5 sts)

Break off yarn and thread through remaining 5 sts and pull together.

Work second finger as follows:

With RS facing, rejoin yarn to remaining sts and pick up 2 sts from base of first finger and K5, turn.

Next row: P12, turn and cast on 2 sts. (14 sts)

Starting with a knit row, work 20 rows of St st on these 14 sts only, ending with a WS row.

Next row: (K1, K2tog) to last 2 sts, K2. (10 sts)

Next row: Purl.

Next row: K2tog to end. (5 sts)

Break off yarn and thread through remaining 5 sts and pull together.

Work third finger as follows:

With RS facing, rejoin yarn to remaining sts and pick up 2 sts from base of second finger and K5, turn.

Next row: P12, turn and cast on 2 sts. (14 sts)

Starting with a knit row, work 18 rows of St st on these 14 sts only, ending with a WS row.

Next row: (K1, K2tog) to last 2 sts, K2. (10 sts)

Next row: Purl.

Next row: (K2tog) to end. (5 sts)

Break off yarn and thread through remaining 5 sts and pull together.

Work fourth finger as follows:

With RS facing, rejoin yarn to remaining sts and pick up 2 sts from base of second finger and K5, turn.

Next row: P12, turn.

Starting with a knit row, work 14 rows of St st, ending with a WS row.

Next row: (K1, K2tog) to end. (8 sts)

Next row: Purl.

Next row: K2tog to end. (4 sts)

Break off yarn and thread through remaining 4 sts and pull together.

Left Hand

Work as for right-hand glove until *.

Shape thumb as follows:

Next row: K20, M1, K3, M1, knit to end. (48 sts)

Next row: Purl.

Next row: K20, M1, K5, M1, knit to end. (50 sts)

Next row: Purl.

Next row: K20, M1, K7, M1, knit to end. (52 sts)

Next row: Purl.

Next row: K20, M1, K9, M1, knit to end. (54 sts)

Next row: Purl.

Next row: K20, M1, K11, M1, knit to end. (56 sts)

Next row: Purl.

Next row: K20, M1, K13, M1, knit to end. (58 sts)

Next row: Purl.

Divide for thumb as follows:

Next row: K35, turn.

Work as for right hand glove from ** to end.

Making up

Sew thumb and finger seams and side seams.

handy

These cosy fingerless gloves are exactly as their name suggests! A striking contrast is created with the mohair and cotton combination.

Materials

Yarn A One 25g ball of Rowan Kidsilk Haze, Colour 600 Dewberry (used double)
Yarn B One 50g ball of Rowan 4 ply Cotton, Colour 127 Flirty (used double)
3.25 mm (US 3) needles
4 mm (US 6) needles

Gauge

22 sts and 30 rows to 4 in. (10 cm) on US 6 (4 mm) needles measured over stocking stitch.

Finished size: to fit average-size adult hand

Right Hand

Cast on 46 sts using A and 3.25 mm (US 3) needles.
Change to B.
Row 1: (RS) (K2, P2) to last 2sts, K2.
Row 2: (WS) (P2, K2) to last 2sts, P2.
Change to A.
Row 3: (K2, P2) to last 2sts, K2.
Row 4: (P2, K2) to last 2sts, P2.
Row 5: (K2, P2) to last 2sts, K2.
Row 6: (P2, K2) to last 2sts, P2.
The last 6 rows form the stripe pattern. Repeat these 6 rows twice more and then repeat rows 1–4 once more.
Change to 4 mm (US 6) needles and B.
Next row: Knit.
Next row: Purl.

Change to A.
Next row: Knit.
Next row: Purl.
Repeat these 2 rows 3 more times.

*Shape thumb as follows:
Next row: K23, M1, K3, M1, knit to end. (48 sts)
Next row: Purl.
Next row: K23, M1, K5, M1, knit to end. (50sts)
Next row: Purl.
Next row: K23, M1, K7, M1, knit to end. (52 sts)
Next row: Purl.
Next row: K23, M1, K9, M1, knit to end. (54 sts)
Next row: Purl.
Next row: K23, M1, K11, M1, knit to end. (56 sts)
Next row: Purl.
Next row: K23, M1, K13, M1, knit to end. (58 sts)
Next row: Purl.

Divide for thumb as follows:
Next row: K38, turn.
Next row: P15, turn.
Starting with a knit row, work 6 rows of St st on
   these 15 sts only, ending with a WS row.
Change to B.
Cast off loosely.

With RS facing, rejoin yarn to remaining sts and
   knit to end. (43 sts)
Next row: Purl.
Next row: Knit.

Next row: Purl.
Repeat last 2 rows 4 more times, ending with a WS
row.

Work first finger as follows:
Next row: K28, turn.
Next row: P13, turn and cast on 2 sts. (15 sts)
Starting with a knit row, work 6 rows of St st on
these 15 sts only, ending with a WS row.
Change to B.
Cast off loosely.

Work second finger as follows:
With RS facing, rejoin yarn to remaining sts and
pick up 2 sts from base of first finger and K5, turn.
Next row: P12, turn and cast on 2 sts. (14 sts)
Starting with a knit row, work 6 rows of St st on
these 14 sts only, ending with a WS row.
Change to B.
Cast off loosely.

Work third finger as follows:
With RS facing, rejoin yarn to remaining sts, pick
up 2 sts from base of second finger and K5, turn.
Next row: P12, turn and cast on 2 sts. (14 sts)
Starting with a knit row, work 6 rows of St st on
these 14 sts only, ending with a WS row.
Change to B.
Cast off loosely.

Work fourth finger as follows:
With RS facing, rejoin yarn to remaining sts, pick
up 2 sts from base of second finger and K5, turn.
Next row: P12, turn.
Starting with a knit row, work 6 rows of St st,
ending with a WS row.
Change to B.
Cast off loosely.

Left Hand
Work as given for right hand glove until *.
Shape thumb as follows:
Next row: K20, M1, K3, M1, knit to end. (48 sts)
Next row: Purl.
Next row: K20, M1, K5, M1, knit to end. (50 sts)
Next row: Purl.
Next row: K20, M1, K7, M1, knit to end. (52 sts)
Next row: Purl.
Next row: K20, M1, K9, M1, knit to end. (54 sts)
Next row: Purl.
Next row: K20, M1, K11, M1, knit to end. (56 sts)
Next row: Purl.
Next row: K20, M1, K13, M1, knit to end. (58 sts)
Next row: Purl.

Divide for thumb as follows:
Next row: K35, turn.
Work as for right hand glove from ** to end.

Making up
Sew thumb and finger seams and side seams.

dizzy

Big, bold polka dots are the main act of these winter mittens and this design is spot on. A striking contrast between the colours further accentuates the strong shapes.

Materials

Yarn A One 50g ball of Rowan Kid Classic, Colour 847 Cherry
Yarn B One 50g ball of Rowan Kid Classic, Colour 844 Frilly
4 mm (US 6) needles
4.5 mm (US 7) needles

Gauge

20 sts and 26 rows to 10 cm (4 in) on 4.5 mm (US 7) needles measured over stocking stitch.

Finished size: to fit average-size adult hand

Right Hand

Cast on 37 sts using B and 4 mm (US 6) needles. Change to A.
Row 1: (RS) K1, (P1, K1) to end.
Row 2: (WS) P1, (K1, P1) to end.
Repeat last 2 rows 7 more times, ending with a WS row.
Change to B and 4.5 mm (US 7) needles.
Next row: (K6, M1) to last 7 sts, K7. (42 sts)
Next row: Purl.
Next row: Knit.
Next row: Purl.

*Starting with chart row 1 and keeping intarsia pattern correct either side of thumb, shape thumb in B as follows:

Next row: K21, M1, K3, M1, knit to end. (44 sts)
Next row: Purl.
Next row: Knit.
Next row: Purl.
Next row: K21, M1, K5, M1, knit to end. (46 sts)
Next row: Purl.
Next row: K21, M1, K7, M1, knit to end. (48 sts)
Next row: Purl.
Next row: K21, M1, K9, M1, knit to end. (50 sts)
Next row: Purl.
Next row: K21, M1, K11, M1, knit to end. (52 sts)
Next row: Purl.

Divide for thumb as follows:
Next row: K34, turn.
**Using only B, work thumb as follows:
Next row: P13, turn.
Starting with a knit row, work 10 rows of St st on these 13 sts only, ending with a WS row.
Next row: K1 (K2tog) to end. (7 sts)
Break off yarn and thread through remaining 7 sts and pull together.
Rejoin yarn at base of thumb and keeping chart pattern correct, inc 3 sts (2A, 1B) and work to end. (42 sts)

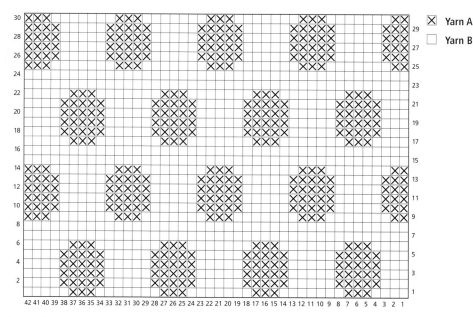

Key: ☒ Yarn A   ☐ Yarn B

Starting with chart row 14, continue without
  shaping following chart until chart row 30 has
  been completed.
Using only B and no longer working from chart,
  shape top as follows:
Next row: K4, K3tog, (K7, K3tog) to last 5 sts, K5.
  (34 sts)
Next row: Purl.
Next row: Knit.
Next row: Purl.
Next row: K3, K3tog, (K5, K3tog) to last 4 sts, K4.
  (26 sts)
Next row: Purl.
Next row: Knit.
Next row: Purl.
Next row: K2, K3tog (K3, K3tog) to last 3 sts, K3.
  (18 sts)
Next row: Purl.
Cast off.

Left Hand
Work as given for right-hand mitten until *.
Next row: K18, M1, K3, M1, knit to end. (44 sts)
Next row: Purl.
Next row: Knit.
Next row: Purl.
Next row: K18, M1, K5, M1, knit to end. (46 sts)
Next row: Purl.
Next row: K18, M1, K7, M1, knit to end. (48 sts)
Next row: Purl.
Next row: K18, M1, K9, M1, knit to end. (50 sts)

Next row: Purl.
Next row: K18, M1, K11, M1, knit to end. (52 sts)
Next row: Purl.
Divide for thumb as follows:
Next row: K31, turn.
Now work as for right-hand mitten from ** to end,
  working inc 3 sts at base of thumb as 3A, instead
  of 2A, 1B.

Making up
Sew side seams, starting at the cast-on edge and
working up the side and across the top.

snug

These very simple-to-knit hand warmers are a great alternative to gloves. The combination of cotton, tweed, and mohair is complemented with a matching button.

Materials

Yarn A One 50g ball of Rowan Felted Tweed, Colour 154 Ginger

Yarn B One 50g ball of Rowan Glace, Colour 739 Dijon

Yarn C One 25g ball of Rowan Kidsilk Haze, Colour 596 Marmalade (used double)

3.25 mm (US 3) needles

3.75 mm (US 5) needles

Two orange buttons (Rowan 00372), 2 cm diameter

Gauge

24 sts and 32 rows to 10 cm (4 in) on 3.25 mm (US 3) needles measured over stocking stitch.

Finished size: to fit average-size adult hand

Right Hand

Cast on 46 sts using C and 3.75 mm (US 5) needles.

Row 1 rib pattern: (RS) K2, (P2, K2) to end.

Row 2 rib pattern: (WS) P2, (K2, P2) to end.

Starting with a RS row, continue in rib pattern as set, working stripes as follows:

1 row in B.

9 rows in A.

1 row in C.

1 row in B.

1 row in C.

9 rows in A.

1 row in C.
1 row in B.
1 row in A.
1 row in C.
1 row in B.
1 row in A.
1 row in C.
1 row in B.
1 row in A.
3 rows in B.
Rest of hand warmer is now worked in St st.
Change to A and 3.25 mm (US 3) needles.
Next row: Knit.
Next row: Purl*.
Shape thumb as follows:
Next row: K23, M1, K3, M1, knit to end. (48 sts)
Next row: Purl.
Next row: K23, M1, K5, M1, knit to end. (50 sts)
Next row: Purl.
Next row: K23, M1, K7, M1, knit to end. (52 sts)
Next row: Purl.
Next row: K23, M1, K9, M1, knit to end. (54 sts)
Next row: Purl.
Next row: K23, M1, K11, M1, knit to end. (56 sts)
Next row: Purl.
Next row: K23, M1, K13, M1, knit to end. (58 sts)
Next row: Purl.

Divide for thumb as follows:
Next row: K38, turn.
**Next row: P15, turn.
Starting with a knit row, work 6 rows of St st on
these 15 sts only, ending with a WS row.
Cast off.

With RS facing, rejoin A at base of thumb to
remaining sts and knit to end. (43 sts)
Next row: Purl.
Next row: Knit.
Next row: Purl.
Repeat last 2 rows twice more, ending with a WS
row.
Change to C.
Next row: Knit.
Next row: Purl.
Next row: Knit.
Repeat last 2 rows twice more, ending with a RS
row.
Next row: Knit. (This creates garter stitch ridge for
turn over at top.)
Next row: Knit.
Next row: Purl.
Next row: Knit.
Next row: Purl.
Cast off loosely.

Left Hand
Work as for right hand until *.
Shape thumb as follows:
Next row: K20, M1, K3, M1, knit to end. (48 sts)
Next row: Purl.
Next row: K20, M1, K5, M1, knit to end. (50 sts)
Next row: Purl.
Next row: K20, M1, K7, M1, knit to end. (52 sts)
Next row: Purl.
Next row: K20, M1, K9, M1, knit to end. (54 sts)
Next row: Purl.
Next row: K20, M1, K11, M1, knit to end. (56 sts)
Next row: Purl.
Next row: K20, M1, K13, M1, knit to end. (58 sts)
Next row: Purl.

Divide for thumb as follows:
Next row: K35, turn.
Work as for right hand from ** to end.

Making up
Turn under the top of each hand warmer along the
garter stitch ridge and slip stitch into place using C.
Sew thumb and side seams. Sew one decorative
button to each cuff.

cosy toes

These ultra-comfy socks will keep your toes warm on the coldest of winter days. A medley of vibrant colours and mohair, wool, and tweed textures have been used to create a cheerful, striped pattern.

Materials

Yarn A Two 50g balls of Rowan 4 ply Soft, Colour 370 Whisper

Yarn B One 50g ball of Rowan 4 ply Soft, Colour 377 Wink

Yarn C One 25g ball of Rowan Kidsilk Haze, Colour 597 Jelly

Yarn D One 25g ball of Rowan Kidsilk Haze, Colour 606 Candy Girl

Yarn E One 25g ball of Rowan Kidsilk Haze, Colour 582 Trance

Yarn F One 25g ball of Rowan Yorkshire Tweed 4 ply, Colour 271 Cheerful

Yarn G One 25g ball of Rowan Yorkshire Tweed 4 ply, Colour 272 Butterscotch

Yarn H One 50g ball of Rowan 4 ply Soft, Colour 379 Goblin

3 mm (US 3) needles

3.25 mm (US 3) needles

Stitch holder

Spare knitting needle

Gauge

28 sts and 36 rows to 10 cm (4 in) on 3.25 mm (US 3) needles measured over stocking stitch.

Finished size: to fit average-size adult foot

Sock (make 2)

Cast on 65 sts using E and (3.25 mm US 3) needles.

Change to A and 3mm (US 3) needles.

Row 1: (RS) K1, (P1, K1) to end.

Row 2: (WS) P1, (K1, p1) to end.

Rep last 2 rows 7 more times, ending with a WS row.

Change to 3.25 mm (US 3) needles.

Starting with a knit row, continue in St st working stripes as follows:

2 rows in H.

1 row in C.

1 row in B.

1 row in D.

1 row in F.

1 row in E.

3 rows in A.

2 rows in H.

2 rows in C.

2 rows in G.

4 rows in B.

4 rows in E.

2 rows in F.

2 rows in A.

6 rows in C.

4 rows in D.

2 rows in B.

6 rows in F.

2 rows in A.

10 rows in H.

10 rows in D.

10 rows in E.

2 rows in A.

10 rows in G.

10 rows in B, ending with a WS row.

Rest of sock is now worked in A only.

Next row: Knit.

Break off yarn.

Shape heel

Slip first 15 sts onto right needle, slip middle 34 instep sts onto a holder, and slip last 16 sts onto a spare needle.

With RS facing, rejoin yarn to instep edge of the 15 sts.

Next row: K14, knit tog next st with first st on spare needle, knit to end. (30 sts)

Next row: Purl.

Next row: Knit.

Rep last 2 rows 7 more times, ending with a RS row.

Next row: Purl.

Turn Heel

K17, K2tog, K1, turn.

P5, P2tog, P1, turn.

K6, K2tog, K1, turn.

P7, P2tog, P1, turn.

K8, K2tog, K1, turn.

P9, P2tog, P1, turn.

K10, K2tog, K1, turn.

P11, P2tog, P1, turn.
K12, K2tog, K1, turn.
P13, P2tog, P1, turn.
K14, K2tog, K1, turn.
P15, P2tog, P2, turn. (18 sts)
Break off yarn.

With RS facing, rejoin yarn and pick up and knit 11 sts down one side of heel, knit 18 sts across heel, and pick up and knit 11 sts up the other side of heel. (40 sts)

Next row: Purl.

Next row: Knit.

Next row: Purl.

Rep last 2 rows once more, ending with WS row.

Next: K1, K2tog tbl, knit to last 3 sts, K2tog, K1. (38 sts)

Next row: Purl.

Next row: Knit.

Next row: Purl.

Next row: K1, K2tog tbl, knit to last 3 sts, K2tog, K1. (36 sts)

Rep last 4 rows twice more, ending with a RS row. (32 sts)

Starting with a purl row, continue in St st until sole measures 20 cm (8 in) from back of heel, ending with a WS row.

Shape toe

Next row: k1, k2tog tbl, knit to last 3sts, k2tog, k1. (30sts)

Next row: Purl.

Next row: K1, K2tog tbl, knit to last 3 sts, K2tog, K1. (28 sts)

Rep last 2 rows twice more, ending with a RS row. (24 sts)

Next row: Purl.

Next row: K1, K2tog tbl, knit to last 3 sts, K2tog, K1. (22 sts)

Next row: P1, P2tog, purl to last 3 sts, P2tog tbl, P1. (20 sts)

Rep last 2 rows until 12 sts remain, ending with a WS row.

Cast off.

Instep

With RS facing, rejoin yarn to 34 sts on holder.

Next row: Knit.

Next row: Purl.

Rep last 2 rows until instep is the same length as sole to toe shaping, ending with a WS row.

Shape toe

Next row: K1, K2tog tbl, k to last 3 sts, K2tog, K1. (32 sts)

Next row: Purl.

Next row: K1, K2tog tbl, knit to last 3 sts, K2tog, K1. (30 sts)

Rep last 2 rows 3 more times, ending with a RS row. (24 sts)

Next row: Purl

Next row: K1, K2tog tbl, knit to last 3 sts, K2tog, K1. (22 sts)

Next row: P1, P2tog, purl to last 3 sts, P2tog tbl, P1. (20 sts)

Rep last 2 rows until 12 sts remain, ending with a WS row.

Cast off.

Making up

Join leg seam. Join instep to sole by working along one side of foot, across the toe and along the other side of foot.

rhubarb

The softest of yarns provide added comfort to these extra-snug ankle-length socks. The pretty picot edging lends a subtle feminine touch.

Materials

Yarn A One 50g ball of Rowan Calmer, Colour 474 Khaki
Yarn B One 50g ball of Rowan Calmer, Colour 477 Blush
4 mm (US 6) needles
4.5 mm (US 7) needles
Stitch holder
Spare knitting needle

Gauge

21 sts and 30 rows to 10 cm (4 in) on 4.5 mm (US 7) needles measured over stocking stitch.

Finished size: to fit average-size adult foot

Sock (make 2)

Cast on using A and 4 mm (US 6) needles as follows:
(Cast on 7 sts, bind off 3 sts, slip stitch on right needle back on to the left needle) 11 times, cast on 2 sts. (46 sts)
Change to B.
Row 1: (RS) (K1, P1) to end.
Repeat this row 7 more times, ending with a WS row.
Change to 4.5 mm (US 7) needles.
Next row: Knit.
Next row: Purl.
Repeat last 2 rows 3 more times, ending with a WS row.

Next row: Knit.
Break off yarn.

Shape heel

Slip first 11 sts onto right needle, slip middle 23 instep sts onto a holder and slip last 12 sts onto a spare needle.

With RS facing, rejoin A to instep edge of the 11 sts.

Next row: K10, knit tog next st with first st on spare needle, knit to end. (22 sts)

Next row: Purl.

Next row: Knit.

Repeat last 2 rows 6 more times, ending with a RS row.

Next row: Purl.

Turn Heel

K13, K2tog, K1, turn.
P5, P2tog, P1, turn.
K6, K2tog, K1, turn.
P7, P2tog, P1, turn.
K8, K2tog, K1, turn.
P9, P2tog, P1, turn.
K10, K2tog, K1, turn.
P11, P2tog, P2. (14 sts)
Break off yarn.

With RS facing, rejoin B and pick up and knit 9 sts down one side of heel, knit 14 sts across heel and pick up and knit 9 sts up the other side of heel. (32 sts)

Next row: Purl.

Next row: Knit.

Next row: Purl.

Next row: K1, K2tog tbl, knit to last 3 sts, K2tog, K1. (30 sts)

Next row: Purl.

Next row: K1, K2tog tbl, knit to last 3 sts, K2tog, K1. (28 sts)

Repeat last 2 rows twice more, ending with a RS row. (24 sts)

Starting with a purl row, continue in St st until sole measures 8 in. (20 cm) from back of heel, ending with a WS row.

Change to A.

Shape toe

Next row: K1, K2tog tbl, knit to last 3 sts, K2tog, K1. (22 sts)

Next row: Purl.

Next row: K1, K2tog tbl, knit to last 3 sts, K2tog, K1. (20 sts)

Rep last 2 rows 3 more times, ending with a RS row. (14 sts)

Next row: P1, P2tog, purl to last 3 sts, P2tog tbl, P1. (12sts)

Cast off.

Instep

With RS facing, rejoin B to 23 sts on holder.

Next row: Knit.

Next row: Purl.

Repeat last 2 rows until instep is the same length as sole to toe shaping, ending with a WS row.

Change to A.

Shape toe

Next row: K1, K2tog tbl, knit to last 3 sts, K2tog, K1. (21 sts)

Next row: Purl.

Next row: K1, K2tog tbl, knit to last 3 sts, K2tog, K1. (19 sts)

Repeat last 2 rows 3 more times, ending with a RS row. (13 sts)

Next row: P1, P2tog, purl to last 3 sts, P2tog tbl, P1. (11 sts)

Cast off.

Making up

Join leg seam. Join instep to sole by working along one side of foot, across the toe and along the other side of foot.

black currant

Looking for a quick knitting fix? Knit with big needles in chunky yarn and this belt is guaranteed to stitch up in a flash! Delicate flowers have been embroidered in a fine cotton and enhanced with a cluster of beads in the centre.

Materials
Yarn A One 100g ball of Rowan Big Wool, Colour 025 Wild Berry
Yarn B One 50g ball of Rowan 4 ply Cotton, Colour 130 Ardour
12 mm (US 17) needles
Approx. 36 mauve beads, 3 mm (J3001020)
Medium crochet hook

Gauge
8 sts and 12 rows to 10 cm (4 in) on 12 mm (US 17) needles measured over stocking stitch.

Finished size: 6 × 78 cm (2½ × 31 in)

Belt
Cast on 5 sts using A and 12 mm (US 17) needles.
Row 1: (RS) (K1, P1) to last st, K1.
This row forms the seed st pattern. Repeat this row 9 more times, ending with a WS row.
Row 11: Knit.
Row 12: K1, P3, K1.
Repeat last 2 rows 4 more times, ending with a WS row.
Rows 21–26: Work as row 1.

Repeat rows 11–20 once more, ending with a WS row.
Continue in seed st as set by row 1 until work measures 19 in. (47 cm) from cast-on edge, ending with a WS row.
Repeat rows 11–26 once and then repeat rows 11–20 once more, ending with a WS row.
Next row: Work as row 1.
Repeat this row 9 more times, ending with a WS row.
Cast off.

Finishing
Using the photograph as a guide, and using B, embroider three daisies (see p.79) onto each of the St st panels. You will have 12 daisies in total. Sew three beads into each of the flower centres.

Tassels (make 10)
Cut ten 60 cm (24 in) lengths of B.
Fold one strand in half, and using a medium crochet hook, thread the folded loop through the corner of the cast-on edge, then fold the ends back through the loop and pull to secure. Do the same at the other corner of the cast-on edge. Attach three more tassels spread evenly in between. Tie all five tassels in a knot at the end. Attach five tassels to the bound-off edge in the same way.

praline

This wide belt is all about texture. Lurex Shimmer loops create a fun three-dimensional knit, and a chunky buckle is used for the fastening.

Materials

Yarn A One 50g ball of Rowan Calmer, Colour 481 Coffee Bean

Yarn B One 25g ball of Rowan Lurex Shimmer, Colour 335 Bronze

Yarn C One 25g ball of Rowan Lurex Shimmer, Colour 330 Copper

4.5 mm (US 7) needles

One brown buckle (Rowan Z075-366), 4 x 6 cm (1½ x 2 in)

Lining fabric, approx. 20 × 80 cm (8 × 32 in)

Gauge

21 sts and 30 rows to 10 cm (4 in) on 4.5 mm (US 7) needles measured over stocking stitch.

Finished size: 10 × 88 cm (4 × 35 in)

Abbreviation

ML Make Loop: Knit into next st and before slipping the st off the left needle, bring yarn to the front of the work between the needle points and wrap around your thumb to create loop and then back through the needle points. Now, knit into the st again and then slip off needle. You will now have two sts on the right hand needle. Bind off one by lifting one over the other. Make sure that when working rows with loops, alternate between B and C. Use C for loops on the first loop row, B for loops on the second loop row, C for loops on the third loop row, and so on.

Belt

Cast on 11 sts using A and on US 7 (4.5 mm) needles.

Row 1: (RS) Knit.

Row 2: (WS) Purl.

Repeat last 2 rows 3 more times, ending with a WS row.

Row 9: Knit.

Row 10: Knit. (This creates garter stitch ridge for turn over hem.)

Row 11: Knit.

Row 12: Purl.

Repeat last 2 rows until work measures 4¾ in. (12 cm) from garter stitch ridge, ending with a WS row.

Next row: K1, M1, knit to last st, M1, K1. (13 sts)

Next row: Purl.

Next row: K1, M1, ML, (K1, ML) to last st, M1, K1. (15 sts)

Repeat last 2 rows until 23 sts, alternating between B and C for loops as described, ending with a WS row.

Next row: K1, ML, (K1, ML) to last st, K1.

Next row: Purl.

Next row: K2, ML, (K1, ML) to last 2sts, K2.

Next row: Purl.

Repeat last 4 rows until work measures 32 in. (80 cm) from cast-on edge, ending with a WS row.

Next row: K2tog, (K1, ML) to last 3 sts, K1, K2tog. (21 sts)

Next row: Purl.

Repeat last 2 rows 3 more times, ending with a WS row. (15 sts)

Next row: K2tog, knit to last 2 sts, K2tog. (13 sts)

Next row: Purl.

Next row: K2tog, knit to last 2 sts, K2tog. (11 sts)

Next row: Purl.

Next row: Knit.

Repeat last 2 rows until work measures 8 cm (3¼ in) from end of loop pattern, ending with a RS row.

Next row: Knit. (This creates garter stitch ridge for turn over hem.)

Next row: Knit.

Next row: Purl.

Repeat last 2 rows 3 more times, ending with a WS row.

Cast off.

Making up

Make fabric lining as follows:

Using the looped area of the belt as a template, cut a piece of lining fabric allowing an extra 1 cm (³⁄₈ in) all a round. Sew a 1 cm (³⁄₈ in) hem all around, as the edges will be seen. Slip stitch the fabric to the back of the belt.

Thread the bound-off edge of the belt around the middle of the buckle, fold the garter stitch ridge over and slip stitch in place. Fold the other end of belt at the garter stitch ridge onto the WS, and slip stitch in place.

COCO

Put your best foot forward – a pair of legwarmers will keep you warm on those chilly mornings. Thick and thin stripes, highlighted with hints of shimmering Lurex, create a look that's fun and youthful.

Materials
Yarn A One 50g ball of Rowan Calmer,
   Colour 480 Peacock
Yarn B One 50g ball of Rowan Calmer,
   Colour 463 Calmer
Yarn C One 50g ball of Rowan Calmer,
   Colour 474 Khaki
Yarn D One 25g ball of Rowan Lurex Shimmer,
   Colour 333 Pewter (used double throughout)
4 mm (US 6) needles
5 mm (US 8) needles

Gauge
19 sts and 27 rows to 10 cm (4 in) on 5 mm
(US 8) needles measured over stocking stitch.

Finished size: 15.75 × 33 cm (6¼ × 13 in)

Legwarmer (make 2)
Cast on 56 sts using A and 4 mm (US 6) needles.
Change to B.
Row 1: (K1, P1) to end.
Repeat last row 11 more times, ending wth a WS
   row.
Change to C and 5 mm (US 8) needles.
Row 13: K7, M1, (K14, M1) to last 7 sts, K7.
   (60 sts)
Row 14: Purl.

Starting with a knit row, continue in St st working
   stripes as follows:
1 row in D.
2 rows in A.
11 rows in B.
2 rows in A.
1 row in D.
2 rows in B.
11 rows in C.
2 rows in B.
1 row in D.
2 rows in C.
11 rows in A.
2 rows in C.
1 row in D.
2 rows in A.
11 rows in B.
2 rows in A.
1 row in D.
2 rows in C, ending with a RS row.
Change to B.
Next row: P6, P2tog, P13, (P2tog, P13) to last 9
   sts, P2tog, P7. (56 sts)
Change to 4 mm (US 6) needles.
Next row: (K1, P1) to end.
Repeat last row 10 more times, ending with a
   RS row.

Change to A.
Next row: (K1, P1) to end.
Cast off in pattern.

Making up
Sew side seams.

lottie

Your feet will be lovely and oh-so-snug in these toasty slippers! Wear them plain or finish them off with a complementary bloom.

Materials

Yarn A Two 50g balls of Rowan Handknit Cotton, Colour 309 Celery

Yarn B One 50g ball of Rowan Kid Classic, Colour 845 Battle

4 mm (US 6) needles

3.25 mm (US 3) needles

4.5 mm (US 7) crochet hook

Gauge

20 sts and 32 rows to 10 cm (4 in) on 4 mm (US 6) needles measured over stocking stitch.

Finished size: to fit average-size adult foot (length can be altered if desired)

First section (make 2)

Cast on 12 sts in A and 15 sts in B using 4 mm (US 6) needles. (27 sts)

Row 1: Using B, K15, using A, sl 1 st purlwise, (K1, P1) to last st, K1.

Row 2: Using A, (K1, P1) 6 times, using B, P15.

Repeat last 2 rows until work measures 14 cm (5½ in), ending with a WS row.

> **note**
> Slipper size can be made smaller or bigger by adjusting the length here.

Next row: (dec) Using B, K2tog, K13, using A, sl 1 st purlwise, K1 (P1, K1) to last 2 sts, K2tog. (25 sts)

Next row: Using A, (P1, K1) 5 times, P1, using B, purl to end.

Next row: Using B, K14, using A, sl 1 st purlwise, (K1, P1) to end.

Next row: Using A, (P1, K1) 5 times, P1, using B, purl to end.

Next row: (dec) Using B, K2tog, K12, using A, sl 1 st purlwise, (K1, P1) to last 2 sts, K2tog. (23 sts)

Next row: Using A, (K1, P1) 5 times, using B, purl to end.

Next row: Using B, K13, using A, sl 1 st purlwise, (K1, P1) to last st, K1.

Next row: Using A, (K1, P1) 5 times, using B, purl to end.

Next row: (dec) Using B, K2tog, K11, using A, sl 1 st purlwise, (K1, P1) 3 times, K1, K2tog. (21 sts)

Next row: Using A, (P1, K1) 4 times, P1, using B, purl to end.

Next row: Using B, K12, using A, sl 1 st purlwise, (K1, P1) to end.

Next row: Using A, (P1, K1) 4 times, P1, using B, purl to end.

Next row: (dec) Using B, K2tog, K10, using A, sl 1 st purlwise, (K1, P1) 3 times, K2tog. (19 sts)

Next row: Using A, (K1, P1) 4 times, using B, purl to end.

Next row: (dec) Using B, K2tog, K9, using A, sl 1 st purlwise, (K1, P1) to last 3sts, K1, K2tog. (17 sts)

Next row: Using A, (P1, K1) 3 times, P1, using B, purl to end.

Next row: (dec) Using B, K2tog, K8, using A, sl 1 st purlwise, (K1, P1) to last 2 sts, K2tog. (15 sts)

Next row: Using A, (K1, P1) 3 times, using B, purl to end.

Next row: (dec) Using B, K2tog, K7, using A, sl 1 st purlwise, K1, P1, K1, K2tog. (13 sts)

Next row: Using A, (P1, K1) twice, P1, using B, purl to end.

Next row: (dec) Using B, K2tog, K6, using A, sl 1 st purlwise, K1, P1 , K2tog. (11 sts)

Next row: Using A, (K1, P1) twice, using B, purl to end.

Next row: (dec) Using B, K2tog, K5, using A, sl 1 st purlwise, K1, K2tog. (9 sts)

Next row: (dec) Using A, K2tog, P1, using B, P3tog, P1, P2tog. (5 sts)

Cast off.

Second section (make 2)

Cast on 15 sts in B and 12 sts in A using 4 mm (US 6) needles. (27 sts)

Row 1: Using A, (K1, P1) 5 times, K1, sl 1 st purlwise, using B, K15.

Row 2: Using B, P15, using A, P1 (K1, P1) 5 times, K1.

Repeat last 2 rows until work measures 14 cm (5½ in), ending with a WS row.

Outer section

Cast on 85 sts using A and 5 mm (US 8) needles.

Row 1: (RS) Knit.

Row 2: (WS) Purl.

Repeat these last 2 rows once more.

Row 5: Knit.

Next row: Knit. (This creates garter stitch ridge for turn over hem.)

Work 4 more rows even, ending with WS row.

Next row: Cast on 4 sts at beg of next 2 rows. (93 sts)

Next row: K4, sl 1, knit to last 5 sts, sl 1, K4.

Next row: Purl.

> ### note
> These last two rows set the stockinette stitch pattern with fifth st in from each end worked as a slipped stitch to create a turn under ridge for hem.

Repeat these last 2 rows, keeping in pattern, until 63 cm (25 in) from cast-on edge, ending with a RS row.

Next row: Cast off 4 sts at beg of next 2 rows. (85 sts)

Next row: Purl.

Next row: Knit.

Next row: Purl.

Next row: Knit.

Next row: Knit. (This creates garter stitch ridge for turn over hem.)

Work 6 more rows even, ending with WS row. Cast off.

Inner section

Cast on 95 sts using B and 4.5 mm (US 7) needles.

Row 1: (RS) Knit.

Row 2: (WS) Purl.

These last 2 rows form St st. Repeat these 2 rows until work measures 63 cm (25 in) from cast-on edge, ending with a WS row. Cast off.

Embroidered pocket

Cast on 26 sts using C and 4 mm (US 6) needles.

Row 1: (RS) Knit.

Row 2: (WS) Purl.

Repeat last 2 rows until pocket measures 21 cm (8½ in), ending with a RS row.

Next row: Knit. (This creates garter stitch ridge for turn over at top of pocket.)

Next row: Knit.

Next row: Purl.

Next row: Knit.

Next row: Purl.

Cast off.

Mkaing up

Using the photograph on page 78 as a guide and D, embroider 8 lazy daisies onto pocket.

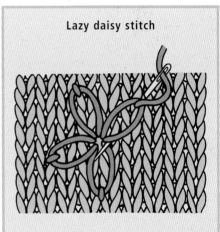

Lazy daisy stitch

This is a method of working individual chain stitches, which are fastened with a small tying stitch, to form 'petals' which can be grouped together to make a 'flower' of 4, 5 or more petals.

Knitting with beads

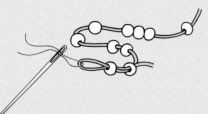
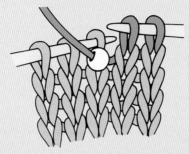
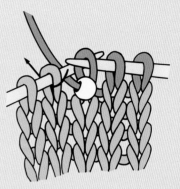

1 Fold a length of sewing cotton in half and thread both ends through a sewing needle. Thread the end of the yarn through the loop in the sewing cotton and fold it back on itself. Thread beads along the needle, down the sewing cotton and onto the yarn until you have the number of beads on the yarn that your pattern requires.

2 On a right side row, knit to the position of the beaded stitch. Bring the yarn forward to the front of the work and push a bead down the yarn close to the last stitch so that it lies over the front of the next stitch.

3 Slip the next stitch purlwise, leaving the bead in front of the slipped stitch. Take the yarn to the back and continue the work as normal.

Beaded pocket

Cast on 19 sts using E and 3.25 mm (US 3) needles.
Row 1: (RS) Knit.
Row 2: (WS) Purl.
Row 3: (K3, PB) to last 3 sts, K3.
Row 4: Purl.
Row 5: Knit.
Row 6: Purl.
Row 7: K5 (PB, K3) to last 6 sts, PB, K5.
Row 8: Purl.
Row 9: Knit.
Row 10: Purl.
Repeat rows 3–10 seven more times, ending with a WS row.
Next row: Work as row 3.
Next row: Purl.
Next row: Knit.

Next row: Knit. (This creates garter stitch ridge for turn over at top of pocket.)
Next row: Knit.
Next row: Purl.
Next row: Knit.
Next row: Purl.
Cast off.

Cabled pocket

Cast on 16 sts using D and 4 mm (US 6) needles.
Row 1: (RS) (K1, P1) twice, K8, (P1, K1) to end.
Row 2: (WS) K1, (P1, K1) twice, P6, K1, (P1, K1) to end.
Repeat last 2 rows once more.
Row 5: K1, (P1, K1) twice, C6B, K1, (P1, K1) to end.
Row 6: K1, (P1, K1) twice, P6, K1, (P1, K1) to end.
Row 7: (K1, P1) twice, K8, (P1, K1) to end.
Row 8: K1, (P1, K1) twice, P6, K1, (P1, K1) to end.

Row 9: (K1, P1) twice, K8, (P1, K1) to end.
Row 10: K1, (P1, K1) twice, P6, K1, (P1, K1) to end.
Row 11: K1, (P1, K1) twice, C6B, K1, (P1, K1) to end.
Repeat rows 6–11 nine more times.
Next row: Work as row 2.
Next row: Work as row 1.
Next row: Knit. (This creates garter stitch ridge for turn over at top of pocket.)
Next row: Knit.
Next row: Purl.
Next row: Knit.
Next row: Purl.
Cast off.

Striped pocket

Cast on 11 sts using F and 3.25 mm (US 3) needles.

Row 1: (RS) Knit.

Row 2: (WS) Purl.

Change to G.

Row 3: Knit.

Row 4: Purl.

The last 4 rows form the stripe pattern. Repeat these 4 rows 15 more times, ending with a WS row.

Change to F.

Next row: Knit.

Next row: Knit. (This creates garter stitch ridge for turn over at top of pocket.)

Next row: Knit.

Next row: Purl.

Next row: Knit.

Next row: Purl.

Cast off.

Garter stitch pocket

Cast on 9 sts using H and 5 mm (US 8) needles.

Row 1: Knit.

This row forms the garter stitch pattern. Repeat row until pocket measures 20 cm (8 in) from cast-on edge, ending with a RS row.

Next row: Knit. (This creates garter stitch ridge for turn over at top of pocket.)

Next row: Knit

Next row: Purl.

Next row: Knit.

Next row: Purl.

Cast off.

Fair Isle chart

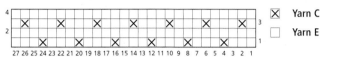

☒ Yarn C
☐ Yarn E

Fair Isle pocket

Cast on 27 sts using E and 3.25 mm (US 3) needles.

Row 1: (RS) Knit.

Row 2: (WS) Purl.

Next, work rows 1–4 of Fair Isle chart. Repeat these 4 chart rows 14 more times, ending with chart row 4 (WS row).

Next row: Knit.

Next row: Knit. (This creates garter stitch ridge for turn over at top of pocket.)

Next row: Knit.

Next row: Purl.

Next row: Knit.

Next row: Purl.

Cast off.

Making up

Lay the outer section on a flat surface with wrong side facing you. Place the inner section on top of the outer section with right side facing. Turn in the knitted hems of the outer section and sew in place. Fold the tops of the pockets at ridge row and sew on WS.

Position the first pocket approx. 7 cm (2¾ in) in from the left-hand edge and 6 cm (2½ in) up from the bottom and sew in place. In the same way position the last pocket approx. 7 cm (2¾ in) in from the right-hand edge and 6 cm (2½ in) up from the bottom and sew in place. Position and sew the remaining four pockets evenly in between.

Cut the ribbon in half. Lay the needle holder on a flat surface with the outside of the outer section facing you. Mark the points to secure the ribbon as follows: measure 13 cm (5¼ in) down from top right corner and place first marker and 13 cm (5¼ in) up from the bottom right hand corner and place a second marker. Measure 10 cm (4 in) to the left of first marker and place a third marker and then 10 cm (4 in) left of that and place a fourth marker. Starting at the second marker, place the fifth and sixth markers in the same way. You now have six points at which to secure the two lengths of ribbon. Allowing 46 cm (18 in) excess of ribbon to hang free at the right-hand side of the holder, sew into place at the marked points. Do the same for the second length of ribbon.

reef

Keep your knitting organised and all your notions in one place with this cabled pencil case with a decorative pom-pom accent. A zip closure ensures that you never mislay a stitch marker or cable needle again!

Materials

One 50g ball of Rowan Denim, Colour 225 Nashville
4mm (US 6) needles
Cable needle
Lining fabric, approx. 30 × 50 cm (12 × 20 in)
One zipper, approx. 18 cm (7¼ in) long
Two circles of cardboard, approx. 2.5 cm (1 in) in diameter
Sewing needle and thread

Gauge

Before washing:
20 sts and 28 rows to 10 cm (4 in) measured over St st using 4 mm (US 6) needles.
After washing:
20 sts and 32 rows to 10 cm (4 in) measured over St st using 4 mm (US 6) needles.

Finished size: 18 × 13 cm (7¼ × 5¼ in)

Abbreviation

C4B Cable 4 Back: Slip next 2 sts onto cable needle and hold at back of work. Knit 2 sts from left needle and then knit the 2 sts from the cable needle.
C4F Cable 4 Front: Slip next 2 sts onto cable needle and hold at front of work. Knit 2 sts from left needle and then knit the 2 sts from the cable needle.

Front

Cast on 32 sts using 4 mm (US 6) needles.
Row 1: K3 (P1, K8) to last 2 sts, P1, K1.
Row 2: (K1, P1, K1, P6) to last 5 sts, K1, P1, K3.
Row 3: K3, P1, K3, C4F, (K1, P1, K3, C4F) to last 3 sts, K1, P1, K1.
Row 4: Work as row 2.
Row 5: K3, (P1, K1, C4B, K3) to last 2 sts, P1, K1.
Row 6: Work as row 2.
Repeat rows 3–6 until work measures 22 cm (8¾ in) from cast-on edge, ending with a WS row. Cast off in pattern.

Back

Cast on 25 sts using 4 mm (US 6) needles.
Row 1: Knit.
Row 2: K3, purl to end.
Repeat last 2 rows until work measures 22 cm (8¾ in) from cast-on edge, ending with a WS row.

Making up

Rowan Denim shrinks in length when washed for the first time, so the front, back, and enough yarn to sew up and to make a pom-pom, must be washed following the instructions on the ball band, before the bag is sewn together.

With the garter stitch edge at the top, use mattress stitch to join the front and back by working down one side, across the bottom and up the other side.

Make fabric lining as follows:
Using the knitted pencil case as a template, cut two pieces of lining fabric slightly larger than the knitted pieces plus 1 cm (⅜ in) all around for the seam allowance. Sew a 1 cm (⅜ in) hem across the top edges of both pieces then sew them together along the other three sides. Turn the pencil case inside out, and with the lining fabric also inside out, sew the bottom two corners of the lining to the bottom two corners of the pencil case. Keeping the lining inside out, turn the pencil case back over it, so it is right side out with the lining inside. With the zipper open, trap the fabric edge of the zipper between the fabric lining and the knitted pencil case and sew into position.

Make pom-pom as follows:
Cut a hole in the center of each circle of cardboard approx. 1½ cm (⅝ in) in diameter. Wind the yarn throught the hole and around the outside of the two circles until the centre hole is almost filled. Cut carefully round the edges of the cardboard until all the yarn has been cut. Ease the pieces of cardboard apart but before taking them off completely, tie a piece of yarn in a secure knot around the centre of the pom-pom to hold It together. Remove the cardboard.Cut an approx. 14 cm (5½ in) length of yarn and fold in half. Sew the two cut ends to the center of the pom-pom, to make a loop. Thread the loop through the zipper pull and folding the pom-pom back through it to secure.

minty

Your mobile phone or ipod will fit snugly inside this cute little cozy. A simple Fair Isle trim has been secured with a large button.

Materials

Yarn A One 50g ball of Rowan Cotton Glace, Colour 809 Pier

Yarn B One 50g ball of Rowan Cotton Glace, Colour 817 Maritime

3.5 mm (US 4) needles

One turquoise button (Rowan 00369), 2.5 cm (1 in) diameter

Gauge

23 sts and 32 rows to 10 cm (4 in) on 3.25 mm (US 3) needles measured over stocking stitch.

Finished size:. 7.5 × 12 cm (3 × 4¾ in)

Front and Back (make one of each)

Cast on 18 sts using B and 3.25 mm (US 3) needles.

Row 1: (RS) Knit.

Row 2: (WS) Purl.

Repeat last 2 rows once more, ending with a WS row.

Row 5: Knit.

Row 6: Knit. (This creates garter st ridge for turn over at top.)

Change to A.

Row 7: Knit.

Row 8: Purl.

Repeat last 2 rows until work measures 14 cm (5½ in) from cast-on edge, ending with a WS row. Bind off.

Belt

Cast on 5 sts using B and 3.25 mm (US 3) needles.

Row 1: Knit.

Row 2: Purl.

Repeat last 2 rows 4 more times, ending with a WS row.

Next, work rows 1 and 2 of chart, below. Repeat these 2 chart rows until work measures 17 cm (6¾ in) from cast-on edge, ending with a chart row 2.

Cast off using B.

Making up

Turn under the top of the front section of the holder along the garter st ridge, and slip stitch into place using B. Do the same for the back. Sew side seams.

Using the photograph as a guide, position the belt around the phone holder and where it overlaps with the section in B on top, sew the button into place neatly and securely.

Yarn A

Yarn B

petal

A colourful corsage adds a dash of feminity to anything, whether as a comely accent to a favorite outfit or an embellishment to other knitted pieces. Give this striking blossom extra dimension by using knitted leaves as a base.

Materials

Yarn A One 50g ball of Rowan Kidsilk Haze, Colour 597 Jelly

Yarn B One 50g ball of Rowan Handknit Cotton, Colour 314 Decadent

Yarn C One 50g ball of Rowan 4 ply Soft, Colour 379 Goblin (used double)

4 mm (US 6) needles

Safety pin

Gauge

22 sts and 30 rows to 10 cm (4 in) on 4 mm (US 6) needles measured over stocking stitch.

Finished size: Flower 6 × 6 cm (2½ × 2½ in)
Including leaves 9 × 9 cm (3½ × 3½ in)

Flower

Cast on 141 sts using A and 4 mm (US 6) needles. Change to B.

Row 1: (RS) K1, (K2, lift first of these sts over second) to end. (71 sts)

Row 2: (WS) P1, (P2tog) to end. (36 sts)

Row 3: K2, (K1, K2tog) to last 4sts, K4. (26 sts)

Row 4: Purl.

Break yarn and thread through remaining sts and pull together. Twist into flower shape and sew to secure.

Small leaf

Cast on 3 sts using C and 4 mm (US 6) needles.

Row 1: (WS) K1, P1, K1.

Row 2: (RS) K1, M1, K1, M1, K1. (5 sts)

Row 3: K1, P3, K1.

Row 4: K2, M1, K1, M1, K2. (7 sts)

Row 5: K1, P5, K1.

Row 6: Knit.

Row 7: K1, P5, K1.

Row 8: K2, sl 2, K1, p2sso, K2. (5 sts)

Row 9: K1, P3, K1.

Row 10: K1, sl 2, K1, p2sso, K1. (3 sts)

Row 11: K1, P1, K1.

Row 12: SL2, K1, p2sso. (1 st)

Fasten off.*

First large leaf

Cast on 3 sts using B and 4 mm (US 6) needles.

Row 1: (WS) K1, P1, K1.

Row 2: (RS) K1, M1, K1, M1, K1. (5 sts)

Row 3: K1, P3, K1.

Row 4: K2, M1, K1, M1, K2. (7 sts)

Row 5: K1, P5, K1.

Row 6: K3, M1, K1, M1, K3. (9 sts)

Row 7: K1, P7, K1.

Row 8: K4, M1, K1, M1, K4. (11 sts)

Row 9: K1, P9, K1.

Row 10: Knit.

Row 11: K1, P9, K1.

Row 12: K4, sl 2, K1, p2sso, K4. (9 sts)

Row 13: K1, P7, k1.

Row 14: K3, sl 2, K1, p2sso, K3. (7 sts)

Row 15: K1, P5, K1.

Row 16: K2, sl 2, K1, p2sso, K2. (5 sts)

Row 17: K1, P3, K1.

Row 18: K1, sl 2, K1, p2sso, K1. (3 sts)

Row 19: K1, P1, K1.

Row 20: Sl2, K1, p2sso. (1 st)

Fasten off.*

> ### note
> When fastening off, leave enough yarn to sew along the length of the petal so that the end can be hidden in the centre of the flower at the back.

Second large leaf

Work as for first large leaf, using C instead of B.

Making up

Sew leaves to back of flower neatly and securely, using the photograph as a guide. Attach a safety pin to back of the corsage.

clematis

Five large petals form this larger-than-life floral brooch. With a cluster of decorative beads and long beaded tassels, this is a must for accessorising!

Materials

Yarn A One 50g ball of Rowan Handknit Cotton, Colour 313 Slick

Yarn B One 25g ball of Rowan Kidsilk Haze, Colour 606 Candy Girl (used double)

3.25 mm (US 3) needles

Approx. 10 large pink beads, 0.5 cm

Safety pin

Gauge

20 sts and 32 rows to 10 cm (4 in) on 3.25 mm (US 3) needles measured over stocking stitch.

Finished size: 12 × 12 cm (4³/₄ × 4³/₄ in)

Large petal (make 5)

Cast on 3 sts using A.

Row 1: (WS) K1, P1, K1.

Row 2: (RS) K1, M1, K1, M1, K1. (5 sts)

Row 3: K1, P3, K1.

Row 4: K2, M1, K1, M1, K2. (7 sts)

Row 5: K1, P5, K1.

Row 6: K3, M1, K1, M1, K3. (9 sts)

Row 7: K1, P7, K1.

Row 8: K4, M1, K1, M1, K4. (11 sts)

Row 9: K1, P9, K1.

Row 10: Knit.

Row 11: K1, P9, K1.

Row 12: K4, sl 2, K1, p2sso, K4. (9 sts)

Row 13: K1, P7, K1.

Row 14: K3, sl 2, K1, p2sso, K3. (7 sts)

Row 15: K1, P5, K1.

Row 16: K2, sl 2, K1, p2sso, K2. (5 sts)

Row 17: K1, P3, K1.

Row 18: K1, sl 2, K1, p2sso, K1. (3 sts)

Row 19: K1, P1, K1.

Row 20: sl 2, K1, p2sso. (1 st)

Fasten off.*

Small petal (make 5)

Cast on 3 sts using B.

Row 1: (WS) K1, P1, K1.

Row 2: (RS) K1, M1, K1, M1, K1. (5 sts)

Row 3: K1, P3, K1.

Row 4: K2, M1, K1, M1, K2. (7 sts)

Row 5: K1, P5, K1.

Row 6: Knit.

Row 7: K1, P5, K1.

Row 8: K2, sl 2, K1, p2sso, K2. (5 sts)

Row 9: K1, P3, K1.

Row 10: K1, sl 2, K1, p2sso, K1. (3 sts)

Row 11: K1, P1, K1.

Row 12: sl 2, K1, p2sso. (1 st)

Fasten off.*

> **note**
> When fastening off, leave enough yarn to sew along the length of the petal so that the end can be hidden in the centre of the flower at the back.

Making up

Using the photograph as a guide, arrange the five large petals into a "star" shape and sew together in the middle to secure. Place the five smaller petals on top of the larger petals and secure in the same way. Sew five beads into the centre of the flower.

Cut five pieces of yarn of varying lengths—approx. 15 cm (6 in), 12 cm (4³/₄ in), 10 cm (4 in), 6 cm (2¹/₂ in) and 4 cm (1¹/₂ in) – and thread a bead onto the end of each one, then secure with a knot. Using the photograph as a guide, and allowing the beads to hang at the front of the flower, sew the five pieces of yarn into the flower centre and secure at the back.

Attach a safety pin to back of the corsage.

zest

A wide Fair Isle band doubles up as a stylish cuff, secured with a large button fastening. This design could be adapted in several ways, such as making it wider, narrower or using a different fastening.

Materials

Yarn A One 50g ball of Rowan Cotton Glace, Colour 787 Hyacinth

Yarn B One 50g ball of Rowan Cotton Glace, Colour 814 Shoot

3.25 mm (US 3) needles

One purple button (Rowan 00374) 2.5 cm (1 in) diameter

Lining fabric, approx. 8 × 18 cm (3¼ in. × 7¼ in)

Sewing needle and thread

Gauge

23 sts and 32 rows to 10 cm (4 in) on 3.25 mm (US 3) needles measured over stocking stitch.

Finished size: 5.5 × 20.5 cm (2¼ × 8¼ in)

Bracelet

Cast on 13 sts using A and 3.25 mm (US 3) needles.

Row 1: (RS) Knit.

Row 2: (WS) Purl.

Repeat last 2 rows once more, ending with a WS row.

Row 5: K5, bind off centre 3 sts, Knit to end.

Row 6: P5, turn, cast on centre 3 sts (see tip), turn, purl to end.

Row 7: Knit.

Row 8: Purl.

Begin working chart rows 1 and 2. Repeat these 2 chart rows until work measures 18 cm (7¼ in) from cast-on edge, ending with chart row 2 (WS).

Continue in A only.

Next row: Knit.

Next row: Purl.

Repeat last 2 rows 3 more times, ending with a WS row.

Cast off.

Making up

Sew button approx. 1.5 cm (⅝ in) in from the bound-off edge.

Make fabric lining as follows:

Using the knitted bracelet as a template, cut out a piece of lining fabric slightly larger than the knitted piece plus 1 cm (⅜ in) all around for the seam allowance. Sew a 1 cm (⅜ in) hem all the way around all four edges, as they will be seen. Slip stitch the fabric to the back of the bracelet, covering all the Fair Isle work and leaving the two ends unlined so button fastening can be used.

13 12 11 10 9 8 7 6 5 4 3 2 1

☐ Yarn A
☒ Yarn B

shimmer

This dazzling necklace is knitted from wire. The beads provide a glittering effect, and long beaded tassels are used as a simple fastening.

Materials

One spool of 28-gauge craft wire
Small amount of Rowan 4 ply Cotton,
   Colour 129 Aegean
One pair 3.25 mm (US 3) double-pointed needles
Approx. 91 turquoise beads, 3mm (J3001013) to fit
   on wire

Finished size: 1 × 31 cm (³/₈ × 12¹/₄ in)
   (excluding ties)

Abbreviation

PB Place Bead: Bring wire forward between needles, slip bead to front of work, sl 1 purlwise, take wire to back of work. Bead will now be sitting in front of the slipped stitch.

Necklace

The necklace is made using a technique sometimes known as either a 'knitted cord' or an 'I-cord.' Once you have cast on your sts you knit one row. Do not turn. Instead, slide the sts to the other end of the double-pointed needle ready to be knitted again. The wire will now be at the left edge of the knitting and so to knit you must pull it tightly across the back of your work and then knit one row. You continue in this way, never turning and always sliding the work to the other end of the double pointed needle; the right side of the work will always be facing you.

Using the technique as described, make the necklace as follows:
Cast on 5 sts using 3.25 mm (US 3) double-pointed needles.
Row 1: (RS) Knit.
Repeat this row 7 more times.
Row 9: K1, PB, K1, PB, K1.
Row 10: Knit.
Row 11: K2, PB, K2.
Row 12: Knit.
Repeat last 4 rows until work measures 28 cm (11 in) from cast-on edge, ending with row 9.
Next row: Knit.
Repeat last row seven more times.
Cast off.

Ties

Cut two 35 cm (14 in) lengths of 4 ply Cotton. Fold one strand in half, then thread the folded loop through the center of the cast-on edge, fold the ends back through the loop and pull to secure. Do the same with the second strand at the center of the bound-off edge. Thread five beads onto the end of each of the strands of cotton, and secure with a knot.

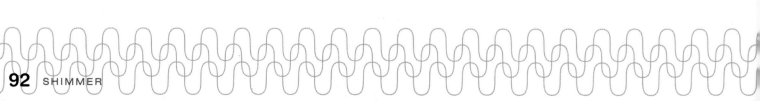

emerald

This beaded wire bracelet has been knitted long enough to wrap around the wrist twice before fastening.

Materials

One spool of 28-gauge craft wire
One pair 3.25mm (US 3) double-pointed needles
Approx. 72 green beads (J3001022) to fit wire
Clasp

Finished size: 0.5 × 40 cm (¼ × 16 in)
   (excluding ties)

Abbreviation

PB Place Bead: Bring wire forward between needles, slip bead to front of work, sl 1 purlwise, take wire to back of work. Bead will now be sitting in front of the slipped stitch.

Bracelet

The bracelet is made using a technique sometimes known as either a 'knitted cord' or an 'I-cord'. Once you have cast on your sts you knit one row. Do not turn. Instead, slide the sts to the other end of the double pointed needle ready to be knitted again. The wire will now be at the left edge of the knitting, so to knit you must pull it tightly across the back of your work and then knit one row. You continue in this way, never turning and always sliding the work to the other end of the double pointed needle; the right side of the work will always be facing you.

Using the technique as described, make the bracelet as follows:
Cast on 3 sts using 3.25 mm (US 3) double
   pointed needles.
Row 1: (RS) Knit.
Row 2: (RS) K1, PB, K1.
Repeat these last 2 rows until work measures
   40 cm (16 in) from cast-on edge.
Next row: Knit.
Cast off.

Making up

Attach clasp to ends of bracelet using wire. Wear bracelet twisted twice around the wrist.

acknowledgements

SUPPLIERS

Emma King: www.emmaking.co.uk

Suppliers of Rowan Yarns
Rowan Yarns
Green Lane Mill
Holmfirth
West Yorkshire
HD9 2DX
Tel: 01484 681881

Suppliers of beads
Beadworks (mail order)
16 Redbridge Enterprise Centre
Thompson Close
Ilford
Essex
IG1 1TY
Tel: 020 8553 3240
www.beadworks.co.uk

The Bead Shop
21a Tower Street
Covent Garden
London
WC2H 9NS
Tel: 020 7240 0931

A big thank you to the following people who have helped to make this book happen:

Rowan for the fantastic yarns which are the inspiration for all I do, in particular to Sharon Brant for her continued support and encouragement; Rita my wonderful knitter and my voice of reason; The entire team at Collins and Brown in particular Katie Cowan and Carly Madden for their help and guidance. Lastly, thank you to my Mum and Pete who are always there caring for me and picking up the pieces when I need them!